AF361604

101

People & Places
That Shaped the
American Revolution
in South Carolina

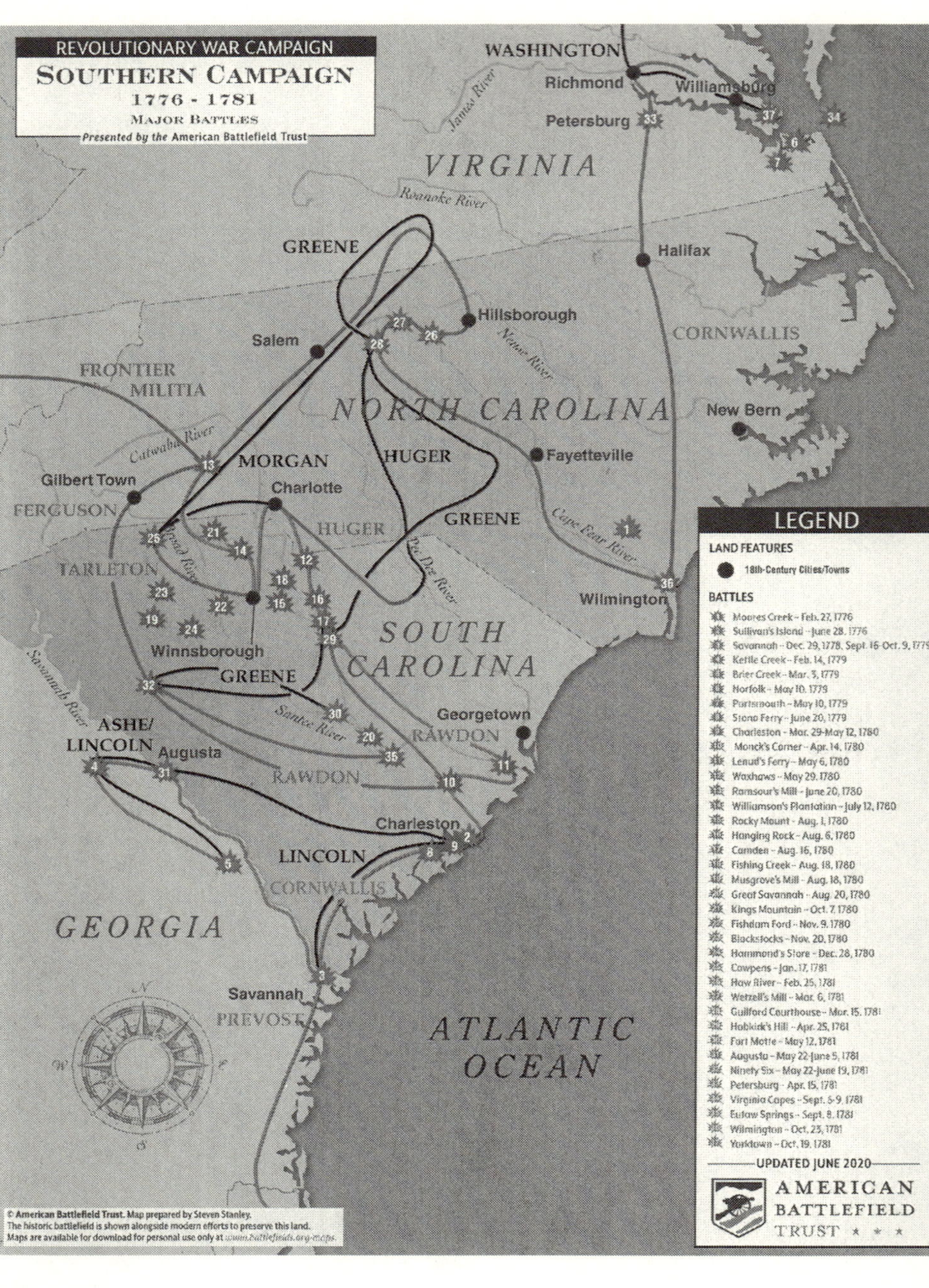

REVOLUTIONARY WAR CAMPAIGN
SOUTHERN CAMPAIGN
1776 - 1781
MAJOR BATTLES
Presented by the American Battlefield Trust

VIRGINIA
WASHINGTON
Richmond
Williamsburg
Petersburg
James River
Roanoke River
GREENE
Halifax
Hillsborough
CORNWALLIS
Salem
Neuse River
NORTH CAROLINA
New Bern
FRONTIER MILITIA
Catawba River
Gilbert Town
MORGAN
Charlotte
HUGER
Fayetteville
FERGUSON
HUGER
GREENE
Cape Fear River
TARLETON
Winnsborough
Pee Dee River
SOUTH CAROLINA
Wilmington
GREENE
Santee River
Georgetown
RAWDON
ASHE/ LINCOLN
Augusta
RAWDON
Savannah River
Charleston
LINCOLN
CORNWALLIS
GEORGIA
Savannah
PREVOST
ATLANTIC OCEAN

N
S
W
E

LEGEND
LAND FEATURES
18th-Century Cities/Towns
BATTLES
Moores Creek – Feb. 27, 1776
Sullivan's Island – June 28, 1776
Savannah – Dec. 29, 1778, Sept. 16-Oct. 9, 1779
Kettle Creek – Feb. 14, 1779
Brier Creek – Mar. 3, 1779
Norfolk – May 10, 1779
Portsmouth – May 10, 1779
Stono Ferry – June 20, 1779
Charleston – Mar. 29-May 12, 1780
Monck's Corner – Apr. 14, 1780
Lenud's Ferry – May 6, 1780
Waxhaws – May 29, 1780
Ramsour's Mill – June 20, 1780
Williamson's Plantation – July 12, 1780
Rocky Mount – Aug. 1, 1780
Hanging Rock – Aug. 6, 1780
Camden – Aug. 16, 1780
Fishing Creek – Aug. 18, 1780
Musgrove's Mill – Aug. 18, 1780
Great Savannah – Aug. 20, 1780
Kings Mountain – Oct. 7, 1780
Fishdam Ford – Nov. 9, 1780
Blackstocks – Nov. 20, 1780
Hammond's Store – Dec. 28, 1780
Cowpens – Jan. 17, 1781
Haw River – Feb. 25, 1781
Wetzell's Mill – Mar. 6, 1781
Guilford Courthouse – Mar. 15, 1781
Hobkirk's Hill – Apr. 25, 1781
Fort Motte – May 12, 1781
Augusta – May 22-June 5, 1781
Ninety Six – May 22-June 19, 1781
Petersburg – Apr. 15, 1781
Virginia Capes – Sept. 5-9, 1781
Eutaw Springs – Sept. 8, 1781
Wilmington – Oct. 23, 1781
Yorktown – Oct. 19, 1781

UPDATED JUNE 2020
AMERICAN BATTLEFIELD TRUST ★ ★ ★

© American Battlefield Trust. Map prepared by Steven Stanley.
The historic battlefield is shown alongside modern efforts to preserve this land.
Maps are available for download for personal use only at www.battlefields.org-maps.

101
People & Places
That Shaped the American Revolution in South Carolina

EDITED BY

Walter Edgar

Published by the University of South Carolina Press
Columbia, South Carolina 29208

www.uscpress.com

Manufactured in the United States of America

30 29 28 27 26 25 24 23 22 21
10 9 8 7 6 5 4 3 2 1

Library of Congress Cataloging-in-Publication Data
can be found at http://catalog.loc.gov/.

ISBN 978-1-64336-227-4 (hardcover)
ISBN 978-1-64336-228-1 (paperback)
ISBN 978-1-64336-229-8 (ebook)

Frontispiece: "Map of the Southern Campaign, 1776–1781."
Reprinted by permission of the American Battlefield Trust (www.battlefields.org).

101 People and Places That Shaped the American Revolution in South Carolina
comprises a compilation of replicated entries from the 2006 edition of
The South Carolina Encyclopedia. Those entries are reproduced here in their
original form. We understand and acknowledge that terminology and
word usage has evolved since the last publication.

Contents

Contents

Illustrations

Preface

The South Carolina Encyclopedia was published in 2006 to be a "people's encyclopedia," a comprehensive single-volume print reference for anything that anyone wanted to know about the Palmetto State's rich cultures and storied heritage, from prehistory to the present. Including nearly two thousand entries and five hundred illustrations, the encyclopedia was the result of a six-year collaboration between the Humanities Council[SC], the Institute for Southern Studies at the University of South Carolina, and the University of South Carolina Press. Nearly six hundred contributors came together to write more than one million words depicting our state's representative people, places, and things. The encyclopedia is an authoritative and entertaining compilation of essays covering an array of topics, ranging from war and politics to arts and recreation, from agriculture and industry to popular culture and ethnicity. As diverse as the populations that live within the thirty-one thousand square miles that make up the Palmetto State, the entries included in *The South Carolina Encyclopedia* were chosen to best represent the many facets of our shared experiences that remind us of who we are, where we come from, what we have in common, and why we are distinctive.

Thanks to the generosity and vision of the Humanities Council[SC] and the collaboration and cooperation of the University of South Carolina Press, selected portions of the multiyear project that became the widely praised and best-selling print encyclopedia are now available in a new way. Drawing from the content of the original print version, *101 People and Places Who Shaped the American Revolution in South Carolina* demonstrates the continued relevance of *The South Carolina Encyclopedia*. It remains an invaluable resource for understanding the state and its people. This volume mines those entries and presents them as a series of essays that tell a collective story.

Because of its thematic focus on a single time period, the era of the American Revolution, this volume expands the accessibility and functionality of the content created in the print encyclopedia and invites new readers to understand better the people and ideas that have defined the South Carolina experience.

Introduction

THE DECISION OF SOUTH CAROLINIANS to leave the British Empire was as much the result of local grievances as it was of changes in imperial policy that occurred after the French and Indian War. At the beginning of the 1770s, the Commons House of Assembly was embroiled in the latest in a series of fierce power struggles with royal officials, known as the Wilkes Fund Controversy. Coupled with new imperial initiatives, these clashes convinced the colony's elite that if it wanted to control the political destiny of South Carolina, then separation was the only answer.

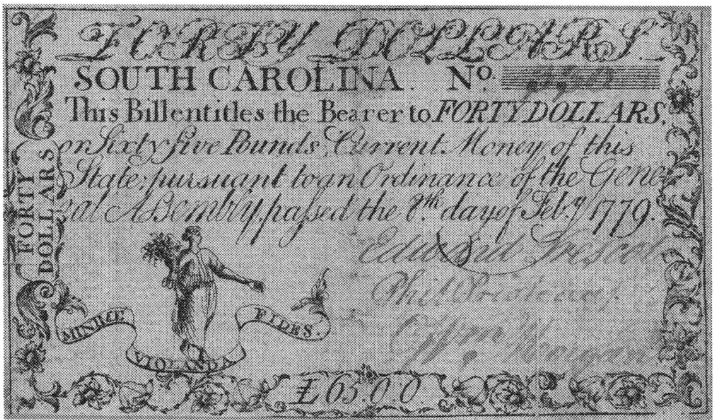

The General Assembly issued paper money to finance the Revolution. Note that the amount on the bill is for forty dollars or sixty-five pounds current money. Courtesy, South Carolina Department of Archives and History.

While the Wilkes Fund Controversy was still boiling, news arrived of the Tea Act granting a monopoly to the British East India Company. In late 1773 the arrival of a ship with a cargo of tea led to the call for a "Mass Meeting" of the populace on December 3. At the meeting, all present agreed to boycott the tea and to establish a committee to enforce the boycott.

The Mass Meeting laid the groundwork for an independent government in South Carolina. At subsequent gatherings, the Mass Meeting established a General Committee to enforce its resolutions and the nonimportation association. When word arrived of the Intolerable Acts—Parliament's response to the Boston Tea Party—South Carolina had in place an organization that could react.

Martha Bratton of York District courted death by refusing to
reveal the whereabouts of her husband's band of partisans.
Courtesy, Historical Center of York County.

When the Boston town meeting asked for assistance and the New York General Assembly suggested an intercolonial congress, the General Committee issued a call for a "General Meeting" of delegates from all corners of the province. The General Meeting, in Charleston on July 6, 1774, adopted a series of resolutions, elected five delegates to the First Continental Congress, and created a Committee of 99 to act on behalf of the General Meeting. This committee quickly became the de facto government of South Carolina as Lowcountry residents responded to the Committee of 99—not the king's appointees. The Commons House fully supported the actions of the General Meeting and appropriated funds for the congressional delegation.

In November 1774, the General Meeting called for the election of a Provincial Congress, which convened in Charleston in January 1775. Over the next nine months, the Provincial Congress and its committees consolidated their hold on the colony. It authorized the seizure of arms and ammunition from royal powder magazines and the State House, the issuing of paper currency to support its operations, the raising of three regiments to defend the colony, and the creation of a Council of Safety with unlimited authority.

Although a majority of congress approved these actions, it was a slim one. Not everyone was ready to make the break with the empire in the summer of 1775; however, the new revolutionary government was in no mood to tolerate dissent. Those who disagreed with congress were dealt with harshly.

The backcountry was a real concern. Nearly two-thirds of the colony's white population resided there, and backcountry residents had more of a beef with the provincial government in Charleston than they did with the British. After backcountry Loyalists ambushed a revolutionary raiding party, congress sent William Henry Drayton and a delegation to the interior settlements, and they achieved an uneasy truce.

While Drayton and his team were in the backcountry, Lord William Campbell, the last royal governor, arrived. He refused to recognize the Provincial Congress as a legitimate body, and a meeting with the Commons House accomplished nothing. In September 1775 Campbell officially dissolved the assembly and fled for his life to a British warship in Charleston harbor. There was no one now to challenge the authority of the Provincial Congress, and it moved swiftly to suppress any opposition.

Renewed tensions in the backcountry led to the mobilization of both Loyalist and patriot militia units. In November 1775, at Ninety Six, there was a skirmish and the first blood of the Revolution in the state was shed. In retaliation, Colonel Richard Richardson raised a force of more than four thousand patriot militiamen to subdue backcountry Loyalists. In what became known as the "Snow Campaign," he defeated the Loyalist militia and tracked down and captured those who had fled.

The new year began with the Provincial Congress in control of all of South Carolina. The backcountry was quiet, and British warships had left Charleston harbor. In March 1776 South Carolina became the first southern colony and the second of the thirteen to draft a state constitution. The Provincial Congress declared itself to be the new General Assembly of South Carolina and elected John Rutledge as president of the state.

South Carolina's new government was concerned with the defense of the state—and with good reason. There were incessant rumors that the British intended to attack Charleston and to incite the Cherokees to invade the frontier settlements. On June 28 a British invasion force launched a combined naval and amphibious assault against revolutionary forces on Sullivan's Island. Led by William Moultrie and William Thomson, the revolutionaries repulsed a British landing force and the sand and palmetto-log fort rendered the naval bombardment ineffective. At the end of the day American casualties were light, and the British withdrew in disarray. The Battle of Sullivan's Island gave a tremendous boost to the revolutionary cause and the upper hand to those who favored a more resolute course of action.

The British fleet remained off Charleston until August. Its presence, and the urging of northern Indian nations, spurred the Cherokees and some Tories to launch a series of raids in July. The response was immediate and brutal. Andrew Williamson led backcountry militia units against the Native Americans, destroyed most of their towns east of the mountains, and then joined with the North Carolina militia to do the same in that state and Georgia. For the remainder of the war, the Cherokees were not a factor.

While the backcountry was subduing the Cherokees, news arrived on August 2 of the Declaration of Independence. That, however, may have been the high tide of revolutionary fervor for a while. After the twin threats of invasion and Indian war had been defeated, the state entered a two-year period of calm that bordered on apathy.

After independence the state needed a new constitution, and a new one was adopted without fanfare in March 1778. Maintaining zeal for the revolution was difficult. So many legislators absented themselves that it was difficult for the General Assembly to meet a quorum. Enlistments declined, and in order to fill its quotas for the Continental army, the legislature offered land and cash bonuses to volunteers. In 1778 the militia law was revised so that one-third of the militia could be slaves (only in support roles). Some black Carolinians, however, were more than engineers or sailors. There were black soldiers in Francis Marion's partisan band and in militia units at King's Mountain and Cowpens.

The lull in the war in the South ended in autumn 1778 when the British captured Savannah. With a base of operations, they could now execute their "southern strategy" to roll up the southern colonies one by one. Throughout 1779 the British made a series of probing attacks against South Carolina almost to the walls of Charleston. In September a French fleet arrived, and the next month the allies launched an unsuccessful attack on Savannah. After the battle the French sailed away, leaving the Americans to fend for themselves.

The new year did not bode well for the American cause in the South. The already thin ranks of the Continentals had been further depleted at Savannah. Benjamin Lincoln, the commander of American forces, under pressure from South Carolina politicians, let himself be convinced that he should move his army behind the walls of Charleston.

Sir Henry Clinton, commander of British forces, brought a large, well-supplied army and a powerful fleet to South Carolina in February 1780. By the end of March, the British army had begun a siege of Charleston and the Royal Navy a blockade by sea. Lincoln's army was trapped.

On April 13 Governor John Rutledge and several members of his council slipped out of the city so that state government could continue. Two months earlier he had been granted extraordinary powers by the General Assembly to prosecute the war. On May 12, 1780, Lincoln surrendered his army of more than 5,500 men. When word of the capitulation reached interior garrisons, they too surrendered.

The capture of Charleston was celebrated throughout the British Empire. But within weeks, blunders by Clinton and his subordinates led to the undoing of his victory. Under the terms of surrender, which applied to civilians as well as military personnel, all adult males were paroled. They agreed that they would not take up arms against the British, and in turn they would not be molested. That suited many Carolinians who simply wanted to go back to their farms and families. However, on June 3 Clinton abrogated the parole of most Carolinians and issued a proclamation that they must take a new oath of allegiance that would require them to take up arms against their fellow Carolinians—something most were loath to do. He then announced the confiscation of the estates of leading revolutionaries and looked the other way as his army plundered the Lowcountry. Encouraged, Tories launched a campaign of retribution.

To solidify his hold on the province, Clinton dispatched units to occupy Ninety Six and Camden. He then left South Carolina for New York, placing Lord Charles Cornwallis in command. Cornwallis ordered his men to "take the most *vigorous* measures to *extinguish the rebellion.*" As they moved into the interior, British troops followed his orders. They executed individuals almost at whim and harassed and maltreated virtually everyone. One commander declared that Presbyterian meetinghouses were "sedition shops" and burned those he encountered. Rather than cowing the populace, these wanton acts of cruelty roused them.

In less than three months, the British and their Tory allies turned what appeared to be a brilliant triumph into a dicey situation. In the northern districts along the North Carolina border, hundreds of Scots-Irish settlers flocked to join partisan bands headed by Thomas Sumter, William Hill, and others. On July 12, 1780, at Williamson's Plantation, partisans defeated elements of the hated British Legion. Over the next ninety days there were sixteen engagements in the northern districts. With the exception of defeats

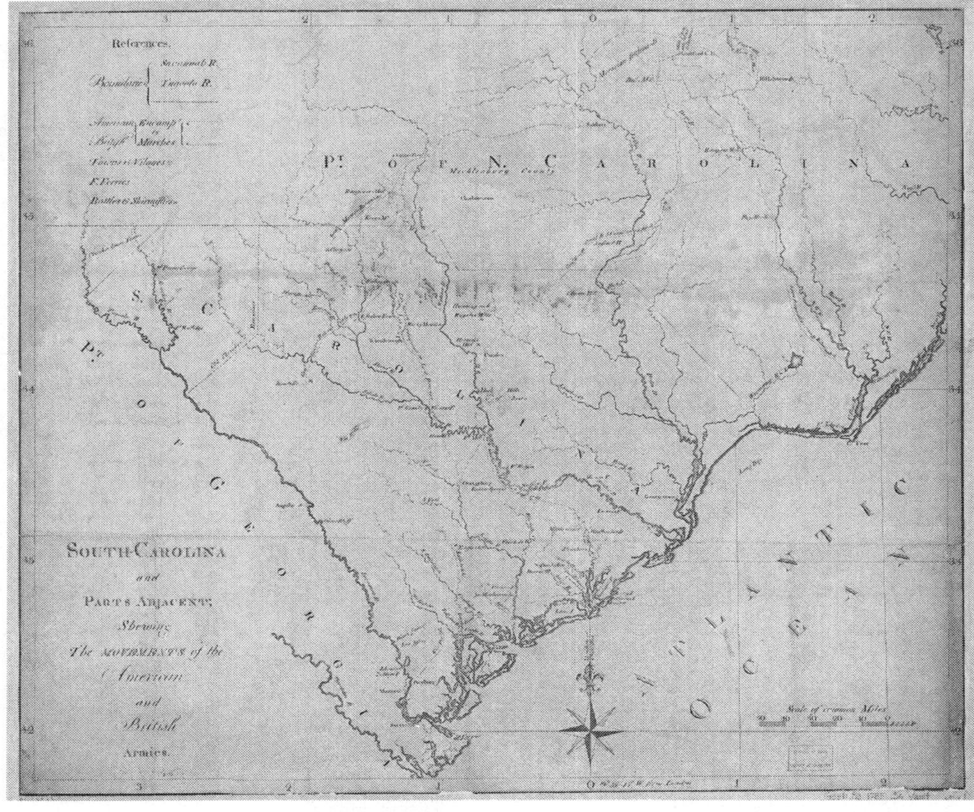

"South Carolina and parts adjacent, shewing the movements of the American and British armies [1781]." From David Ramsay, History of the Revolution of South Carolina. Charleston, SC: 1785. Courtesy, Library of Congress, Geography and Map Division.

at Camden and Fishing Creek, the remainder were all partisan victories culminating in the smashing victory at King's Mountain. Losing more than one thousand soldiers killed, wounded, or captured so unnerved the British that Cornwallis delayed a planned invasion of North Carolina.

The situation deteriorated throughout the remainder of the year as partisans attacked isolated outposts and supply trains. Francis Marion operated at will in the northeastern portion of the state. Andrew Pickens led forces in the Savannah River Valley, and William Harden did the same in the Lowcountry south of Charleston. Thomas Sumter continued his operations in the central and northern districts.

On December 14, 1782, Gen. Nathanael Greene led patriot forces into Charleston, ending a brutal British occupation of thirty-one months. (Nathanael Greene, National Portrait Gallery, Smithsonian Institution)

In December, Nathanael Greene appeared with a new Continental army. It was a turning point in the war. Unlike most regular military men who disliked and dismissed partisans, Greene coordinated their efforts with his own and kept the British continually off balance. By trading space for time, he planned a war of attrition that would eventually defeat a superior enemy force.

Shortly after his arrival in South Carolina, he divided his command, sending a large detachment under Daniel Morgan toward Ninety Six. As he had hoped, Cornwallis divided his army. On January 17, 1781, Morgan made a stand on the Broad River in Spartan District at Hiram Sanders's cowpens. For the first time in the Revolution, a regular British force broke and ran. Nearly one thousand of the enemy were killed or captured along with most of their supplies. The successful partisan operations, coupled with the victories at King's Mountain and Cowpens, had turned the tide in South Carolina in the Americans' favor. But the war had not yet been won.

After Cowpens, Morgan moved swiftly into North Carolina to rejoin Greene's main army with Cornwallis right behind him. Eventually, after racing to the Dan River, Greene doubled back to Guilford Courthouse, where he engaged the British. When the fighting ended, the British held the field, but they had suffered heavy casualties. Cornwallis withdrew his tattered army to Wilmington and from there marched north to Virginia.

Greene headed back to South Carolina. Facing him was a combined regular-Loyalist force of about eight thousand stationed in Charleston and at outposts from Georgetown to Ninety Six. The British may have controlled the strong points, but the countryside belonged to the partisans. With Greene's army to keep the main British forces occupied, the partisans picked off the enemy garrisons one by one.

During the spring and summer of 1781 there were three major battles in the state. On April 25 at Hobkirk's Hill, the British won the battle but withdrew their garrison from Camden. At Ninety Six, Greene conducted an unsuccessful siege from May 22 to June 19, but the British abandoned the fort in June. At Eutaw Springs on September 8, in what was the bloodiest battle of the southern campaign, Greene initially held the field, but the British counterattacked and, at the end of the day, drove the Americans back. There were other battles after Eutaw Springs, but none of any strategic significance. On November 14, 1782, the last of the 137 battles fought in South Carolina and the last battle of the American Revolution occurred on Johns Island.

Because the British still occupied Charleston in January 1782, the General Assembly met in Jacksonborough. Under the protection of Greene's army, the legislature elected a new governor and passed two acts identifying and punishing Loyalists. The state was able to reassert its authority everywhere except for James Island and the Charleston peninsula.

In September 1782 a British fleet sailed into Charleston harbor to transport the remaining troops and the 4,200 Loyalists who wished to leave the state. On December 14, 1782, the last of the occupying troops withdrew block by block, and the city was turned over to Greene's army. At 3:00 p.m. Greene escorted Governor John Mathewes and other officials into the city. For South Carolina, the war was over.

After thirty months of bloody fighting and brutal occupation, South Carolinians were once again in control of their own affairs—thanks to Nathanael Greene and local partisan leaders. The war may have begun and ended in Charleston, but it was won in the forests and swamps of the backcountry.

A nineteenth-century engraving of the Battle of Eutaw Springs, the
last major engagement of the Revolution in South Carolina.
Courtesy, New York Public Library.

From Ninety Six to Charleston the countryside was in ruins. Dwellings,
farm buildings, and mills had been burned. Fields had been abandoned and
had become overgrown. Livestock had been taken by one side or the other.
There were thirty thousand fewer slaves in the state than there had been in
1775. The state's economy was in shambles.

Not only were the means of production damaged or destroyed, but individuals and the state faced huge debts. South Carolina, with a white population of less than 100,000, had spent $5.4 million on the war effort. In spite of
the difficulties facing it, the state had regularly met its financial obligations
to the Continental Congress. In 1783 it was the only state to pay its requisi-
tion in full. The financial losses were nothing compared to the personal ones.
In 1783 a visitor noted the large number of widows in Charleston, but there
were far more in the backcountry. In Ninety Six District it was estimated that
there were at least twelve hundred widows.

The American Revolution in South Carolina was a bloody, desperate
struggle—America's first civil war. Because of the nature of the conflict, it is
impossible to know exactly how many Carolinians perished. However, of the

total number of American casualties for the entire war, 18 percent of those killed and 31 percent of those wounded fell in South Carolina during the last two years of fighting. Given the material and human losses, it is no small wonder that the American historian George Bancroft would write: "Left mainly to her own resources, it was through the depths of wretchedness that her sons were to bring her back to her place in the republic . . . having suffered more, and dared more, and achieved more than the men of any other state."

Buchanan, John. *The Road to Guilford Courthouse: The American Revolution in the Carolinas.* New York: Wiley, 1997.
Edgar, Walter. *Partisans and Redcoats: The Southern Conflict That Turned the Tide of the American Revolution.* New York: Morrow, 2001.
McCrady, Edward. *The History of South Carolina in the Revolution.* 2 vols. New York: Macmillan, 1901–1902.

AFRICAN AMERICANS IN THE REVOLUTIONARY WAR. African Americans contributed to both the American and British causes during the Revolutionary War as laborers, soldiers, sailors, guides, teamsters, cooks, and spies. While it is impossible to know the exact number, it has been traditionally accepted that as many as five thousand African Americans served in the American forces. Perhaps as many as 80,000 to 100,000 slaves either escaped during the war, were taken by the British, or fled with Loyalists and British soldiers afterward. A few hundred of these served in the British ranks. African Americans joined the American or British armies under many different motives and circumstances. Slaves joined when promised freedom for their service, or were seized by one side or the other, or served as substitutes for their owners. Slaveowners were sometimes paid for the labor their slaves provided, but in other instances slaves were seized as military necessity required. Free blacks joined to enhance their status in the community or for monetary reward. When serving as soldiers, African Americans were usually integrated into the ranks. However, the colonies raised a few segregated regiments such as the First Rhode Island Regiment and the black regiment raised by Governor Lord Dunmore of Virginia for the British.

At the beginning of the war, South Carolina patriots attempted to keep slaves on the plantations by passing a law instituting the death penalty for any slave who joined the British. Meanwhile, two South Carolina delegates to the Continental Congress, Edward Rutledge and Thomas Lynch, worked to have the free African Americans who had joined the ranks of the Continental army discharged and excluded from any future enlistments. But other South Carolinians such as Henry and John Laurens were in favor of African Americans serving and of giving slaves their freedom in exchange for military service. Congress even sent John Laurens on a mission to South Carolina in 1779 in hopes of convincing the state to raise three thousand blacks for segregated battalions to be led by white officers. Under this proposal, Congress would pay plantation owners for the slaves recruited into the battalions. The slaveowners would get up to $1,000 for each able-bodied black male under thirty-five years of age, and at the war's conclusion the slave would receive his freedom and $50. The South Carolina legislature quickly rejected the idea. Later, in 1781, they rejected another request by General Nathanael Greene to raise black troops. However, South Carolina slaves were used as bounty to raise white recruits. In 1781 General Thomas Sumter offered one slave to each white citizen who joined as a private soldier for ten months and as many as three grown and one small slave to those who joined as colonels. Sumter did not have these slaves at the time he made this promise. He was banking on slaves he hoped would be seized from Loyalists during future campaigns. General Andrew Pickens also adopted this recruiting incentive, which became known as "Sumter's law," but Francis Marion rejected it, stating that it was "inhuman."

While most African Americans who served in South Carolina, slave or free, were laborers, cooks, or teamsters in the war, a few were combatants. Their presence in the ranks is only known from incidental comments found in contemporary diaries and correspondence. For instance, when Francis Marion crossed into North Carolina to join General Horatio Gates during the summer of 1780, Otho Williams recorded that Marion's men "did not exceed twenty men and boys, some white, some black, and all mounted, but most of them miserably equipped." Once, the South Carolina legislature rewarded a slave named Antigua for his role as an American spy. While the number of African Americans in the South Carolina lines may have been small, blacks made up a significant portion of the crews on South Carolina's ships during the war. African Americans were common in South Carolina's navy, serving as seamen, pilots, and carpenters.

At the end of the war, as many as 25,000 South Carolina slaves left with the British and Loyalists or escaped into the swamps. One band of three hundred Georgia and South Carolina slaves, who called themselves King of England's Soldiers, fled to the Savannah River swamps and survived until May of 1786, when they were burned out by Georgia and South Carolina militia. STEVEN D. SMITH

Foner, Philip S. *Blacks in the American Revolution.* Westport, Conn.: Greenwood, 1976.
Nalty, Bernard C. *Strength for the Fight: A History of Black Americans in the Military.* New York: Free Press, 1986.
Quarles, Benjamin. *The Negro in the American Revolution.* 1961. Reprint, Chapel Hill: University of North Carolina Press, 1996.

BARRY, MARGARET CATHERINE MOORE (1752–1823). Revolutionary War heroine. "Kate" Barry was born Margaret Catherine Moore in county Antrim, Ireland, the daughter of Charles and Mary Moore. In 1763 her father received a land grant in South Carolina, which eventually became Walnut Grove plantation in Spartanburg County. She married Andrew Barry (ca. 1744–1811), and they lived at Walnut Grove.

During the Revolutionary War, Andrew Barry served as a captain in the militia under Major Henry White and Colonel John Thomas, Jr. Before the engagement in January 1781 that became known as the Battle of Cowpens, General Daniel Morgan sent messages through the countryside to summon the militia to muster and join his army. Kate Barry helped carry the call to arms by riding through the neighborhood. She also served as a scout for the patriot forces. When captured, she refused to reveal the position of her husband's company, and some accounts reported that the British beat her in retaliation.

Kate Barry's ride before the Battle of Cowpens was memorialized in poetry and monuments. Her activities not only helped patriot forces, but also served as anti-British propaganda. Regardless of whether the story of British brutality was true, the story was used as support for the case against the British military in the South. Kate Barry died in 1823 and was buried in the cemetery at Walnut Grove. BRENDA THOMPSON SCHOOLFIELD

Babits, Lawrence E. *A Devil of a Whipping: The Battle of Cowpens.* Chapel Hill: University of North Carolina Press, 1998.
Moss, Bobby Gilmer. *The Patriots at the Cowpens.* Greenville, S.C.: A Press, 1985.

BRATTON, WILLIAM (ca. 1742–1815). Soldier, legislator. Bratton was born in county Antrim, Ireland, and immigrated with his family to America not long afterward. Family traditions recorded in the nineteenth century stated that Bratton lived in Pennsylvania, Virginia, and North Carolina before moving to South Carolina in the 1760s. Beginning in 1765, an extended family of Brattons—including John, Robert, Thomas, Hugh, and William Bratton—moved into the area of present-day York County as part of a larger migration of Scots-Irish into the Carolina Piedmont immediately after the French and Indian War. William Bratton probably married his wife, Martha Robinson or Robertson (ca. 1750–1816), about this same time. They had eight children. In 1766 Bratton purchased two hundred acres of land on the South Fork of Fishing Creek. The Brattons' original two-story log house, which probably dates from this same period, still exists as the Colonel William Bratton House at Historic Brattonsville in York County.

During the Revolutionary War, Bratton served as a South Carolina militia commander and rose from the rank of captain at the beginning of the war to colonel by late 1780, when he commanded a regiment in the partisan brigade of General Thomas Sumter. Early on the morning of July 12, 1780, an important battle was fought near Bratton's home on the neighboring plantation of James Williamson this battle is today known as the Battle of Williamson's Plantation or, locally, as Huck's Defeat. A force of about 133 local militiamen under the command of Bratton, William Hill, John McClure, Edward Lacey and others ambushed and defeated a mixed force of about 120 British Provincials and Loyalist militia under the command of Captain Christian Huck of the British Legion. This battle was the first significant defeat of British forces by South Carolina militia after the surrender of Charleston in May 1780, and it revitalized the patriot cause in the upstate.

Bratton served as a regimental commander in Sumter's Brigade until the end of the Revolution. After the war, he served as a justice of the peace for York County, sheriff of Pinckney District, and a state legislator in both the House of Representatives (1785–1790) and the Senate (1791–1794). He also operated a small store, was a successful planter and businessman, and owned several slaves. William and Martha Bratton were early members of Bethesda Presbyterian Church, one of the oldest churches in the region. Bratton died on February 9, 1815, and was buried in the Bethesda Presbyterian Church cemetery. His children and grandchildren expanded the homesite into a large nineteenth-century plantation, which became known as the village of Brattonsville. MICHAEL C. SCOGGINS

Bailey, N. Louise, and Elizabeth Ivey Cooper, eds. *Biographical Directory of the South Carolina House of Representatives.* Vol. 3, *1775–1790.* Columbia: University of South Carolina Press, 1981.

Moore, Maurice A. *Reminiscences of York.* Edited by Elmer O. Parker. Greenville, S.C.: A Press, 1981.

BROWN, THOMAS (1750–1825). Soldier. Brown was among the most notorious Loyalist commanders in the South during the Revolutionary War. He was born on May 27, 1750, in Whitby, England. Having acquired large tracts of the "Ceded Lands" near Augusta, Georgia, he immigrated to Georgia in the autumn of 1774. Brown promptly established a sizable plantation and became involved in local politics, particularly in expressing his opposition to the revolutionary movement. On August 2, 1775, a committee of the local Sons of Liberty seized and tortured him when Brown refused to renounce allegiance to his king. Making an escape, he fled to the South Carolina backcountry where he joined an active group of Loyalists. He set to work against the commission sent to the interior by the Charleston Council of Safety to gain support for the American effort and assisted in organizing an armed Loyalist force. Brown was among the Tory leaders at a confrontation with a rebel force near Ninety Six in September 1775. After a truce, he went to Charleston to confer with South Carolina's royal governor Lord William Campbell but was arrested by the Council of Safety and ordered to leave Charleston.

Finding refuge in British-held St. Augustine, Florida, Brown was commissioned a lieutenant colonel in June 1776 by East Florida's royal governor Patrick Tonyn and authorized to raise a regiment of mounted rangers. In the early years of the war, the rangers and their Creek and Cherokee allies patrolled the Georgia–South Carolina frontier. By 1779 the British held most of Georgia, which made East Florida's security seem certain. Brown's regiment was deactivated in June and reorganized as the King's Carolina Rangers, a regular provincial corps. That same month he was appointed one of two British superintendents of the Southern Indian Department, thereby putting Creek and Cherokee relations under his control.

At the onset of 1780, Brown established his headquarters at Augusta and directed the activities of Tories and Indians against the patriots. He was wounded in an attack on the town in mid-September 1780 by an American force commanded by Elijah Clarke. After the unsuccessful siege, Brown ordered thirteen prisoners hanged for parole violations. A second siege, led by Colonel Henry Lee of the Continental army and General Andrew Pickens of the South Carolina militia, forced Brown to submit on June 5, 1781. After being exchanged, Brown made his headquarters as Indian superintendent in Savannah, until the evacuation of that city by the British in July 1782, and then in St. Augustine. Following the return of Florida to Spain, he moved to the Bahamas to start life anew. In one of David Ramsey's histories of the war, Brown wrote an impassioned defense of his conduct in reply to charges of cruelty. Brown died on his St. Vincent Island plantation on August 3, 1825. SAMUEL K. FORE

Cashin, Edward J. *The King's Ranger: Thomas Brown and the American Revolution on the Southern Frontier.* Athens: University of Georgia Press, 1989.

Lambert, Robert Stansbury. *South Carolina Loyalists in the American Revolution.* Columbia: University of South Carolina Press, 1987.

Olson, Gary D. "Dr. David Ramsay and Lt. Colonel Thomas Brown: Patriot Historian and Loyalist Critic." *South Carolina Historical Magazine* 77 (October 1976): 257–67.

———. "Loyalists and the American Revolution: Thomas Brown and the South Carolina Backcountry, 1775–1776." *South Carolina Historical Magazine* 68 (October 1967): 201–19; 69 (January 1968): 44–56.

BULL, STEPHEN (?–1800). Soldier, legislator. Bull was born in South Carolina, the only surviving son of Stephen Bull and Martha Godin. He was descended from one of the first families of colonial South Carolina and was the nephew of Lieutenant Governor William Bull II. Bull inherited Sheldon Plantation in Prince William's Parish. His family's prominence thrust him into political leadership. He represented Prince William's in the Commons House of Assembly from 1757 to 1760 and served as a justice of the peace from 1756 to 1769.

On the eve of the Revolutionary War, Bull was the colonel commanding the Beaufort District militia regiment. Unlike most members of his family, Bull supported the American cause and took up arms against the king. He led his regiment in the occupation of Savannah in 1776, a decisive event in bolstering Georgia patriots and driving Loyalists from Savannah. In 1778 Bull was promoted to brigadier general and led his regiment in the ill-fated American campaign against British East Florida. Command of the American forces was divided between General Robert Howe of the Continental army and Governor John Houston of Georgia. The American army never got past the Loyalist fort at St. Mary's, Georgia.

Bull participated with General William Moultrie in the American victory at Port Royal Island on February 3, 1779. Two months later the Lowcountry was overrun by British General Augustine Prevost's invasion from Georgia, and defeat and desertions decimated Bull's regiment. After the fall of Charleston in May 1780, Bull went into self-imposed exile in Virginia and Maryland and offered no more service to the patriot cause.

Politically, Bull was elected from Prince William's Parish to the First and Second Provincial Congresses in 1775 and 1776 and the First and Second General Assemblies of South Carolina from 1776 to 1778. After the war Bull was a member of the S.C. House of Representatives from 1783 to 1790. He was twice elected to the S.C. Senate but declined to serve.

Bull was married first to Elizabeth Woodward, on December 18, 1755, and then to Ann Barnwell, on May 24, 1772. By his second wife he had three daughters: Charlotte, Mary, and Sarah. Bull died in 1800 and was buried at the ancestral seat at Ashley Hall, but he was later interred in Magnolia Cemetery, Charleston. LAWRENCE S. ROWLAND

Bailey, N. Louise, Mary L. Morgan, and Carolyn R. Taylor, eds. *Biographical Directory of the South Carolina Senate.* 3 vols. Columbia: University of South Carolina Press, 1986.

"Bull Family of South Carolina." *South Carolina Historical and Genealogical Magazine* 1 (January 1900): 76–90.

Rowland, Lawrence S., Alexander Moore, and George C. Rogers. *The History of Beaufort County, South Carolina.* Vol. 1, *1514–1861.* Columbia: University of South Carolina Press, 1996.

BULL, WILLIAM, II (1710–1791). Lieutenant governor. Bull was born on September 24, 1710, at Ashley Hall Plantation, the son of William Bull (1683–1755) and Mary Quintyne. He was educated in London, England, at Westminster School and received an M.D. degree at Leyden University in the Netherlands. Bull was the first native-born American to earn a doctor of medicine degree. He did not establish a professional medical practice, but rather had a prolific career as a planter-politician.

Bull followed his father into politics when he was elected to the Commons House of Assembly for St. Andrew's Parish (1736). For thirteen years he represented St. John's Berkeley, St. Bartholomew's, and Prince William's Parishes. While a member and occasional Speaker of the House, he collaborated with his father, a member of the Royal Council, to expand colonial authority. In 1749 he joined the Royal Council. Ten years later, in 1759, Bull became president of the Council and lieutenant governor, and he held that post until his political career ended in 1775. During that period he was acting governor on five occasions, for a total of eight years of service. Bull opposed William Henry Lyttelton's Cherokee War policies, and when Lyttelton left the province in 1760, Bull started negotiations to end the war.

Bull's second term as acting governor (1764–1766) coincided with the Stamp Act crisis in the American colonies. He was not a strong supporter of the act but dutifully performed his job as a royal appointee. He clashed with radical members of the Commons House, including his brothers-in-law, Henry Middleton and John Drayton, and suffered the opprobrium of Charleston's Sons of Liberty. Despite difficulties, he was able to steer a course between the opposing factions. He negotiated the reopening of the Port of Charleston and the colonial courts, which had been closed by boycotts and the fear of mob violence if tax stamps were sold. Bull encouraged the expansion of the colony into the backcountry. As lieutenant and acting governor, he took a conciliatory approach to the Regulator movement and supported the creation of new parishes (election districts), schools, and courts in the backcountry.

During the 1770s Bull's political views grew increasingly out of step as South Carolina and other colonies moved toward radical opposition to the crown. The year 1775 was one of crisis in Bull's life and in the independence movement in South Carolina. Henry Middleton was president of the Continental Congress in Philadelphia, and the Provincial Congress of South Carolina began to organize for independence. Its Council of Safety, which included among its members Henry Laurens, William Henry Drayton, and Arthur Middleton, planned to take over the executive duties of a revolutionary government. Lord William Campbell, the last royal governor, arrived at Charleston on June 18, 1775, and took office, but his term lasted only three months. On September 15 he was forced to flee the city for refuge on a British warship in Charleston harbor. The revolution was under way, and Bull's position was an impossible one. He resigned from the Royal Council and retired to his Ashley Hall plantation. In 1777 he refused to take the oath of allegiance to the revolutionary government and was banished from the state. He executed deeds of trust and powers of attorney to his nephew Stephen Bull and other revolutionaries for his properties, then left for England on May 4, 1777.

Charleston was captured by British forces in May 1780, and in February 1781 Bull returned home. He became intendant general on the Board of Police, the body that governed occupied Charleston. He vainly sought clemency for the captured patriot Colonel Isaac Hayne, who was hanged by the British for breaking his parole. Despite his mediating actions, the General Assembly ordered Bull's property confiscated as punishment for his collaboration with the occupiers. His plantations, slaves, and personal property were appraised at £51,554 sterling. When the British evacuated Charleston in December 1782, Bull sailed back to England into a second, permanent exile. Despite his efforts to return to South Carolina after the Revolution, he was unsuccessful. He recovered his properties, and his name was removed, post facto, from the list of banished Loyalists. William Bull died in London on July 4, 1791, and was buried in St. Andrews Holburn Church, London. He was survived by his wife, Hannah Beale, daughter of Othniel Beale, whom he had wed on August 17, 1746. The couple had no children, and his considerable estate was divided among the children of his siblings. ALEXANDER MOORE

Bull, Kinloch, Jr. *The Oligarchs in Colonial and Revolutionary Charleston: Lieutenant Governor William Bull II and His Family.* Columbia: University of South Carolina Press, 1991.

Edgar, Walter, and N. Louise Bailey, eds. *Biographical Directory of the South Carolina House of Representatives.* Vol. 2, *The Commons House of Assembly, 1692–1775.* Columbia: University of South Carolina Press, 1977.

Meroney, Geraldine M. *Inseparable Loyalty: A Biography of William Bull.* Norcross, Ga.: Harrison, 1991.

Sirmans, M. Eugene. "Masters of Ashley Hall: A Biographical Study of the Bull Family of Colonial South Carolina, 1670–1737." Ph.D. diss., Princeton University, 1959.

CAMDEN, BATTLE OF (August 16, 1780). In early April 1780, as British forces tightened their grip around Charleston, the Maryland Division, the Delaware Regiment, and the First Continental Artillery Regiment received orders to march for the Southern Department, where they were expected to serve as the main component of a Charleston relief expedition. With the fall of Charleston on May 12, this element of the Continental army, under the command of Major General Baron Johann de Kalb, became the only significant force in the South. The Continental Congress, however, felt that the crisis deserved a more illustrious savior and appointed Major General Horatio Gates, the hero of the Saratoga campaign, to command the Southern Department. He arrived in de Kalb's camp at Buffalo Ford in North Carolina on July 25.

The new commander resolved to advance on the British outpost at Camden, South Carolina. De Kalb agreed but suggested taking the route via Salisbury and Charlotte through friendly country in order to obtain food and supplies for the army. Gates instead chose a direct march to catch the British garrison by surprise. The "grand army" (as Gates called his force) set out immediately on July 27 on a long and weary march with little to eat. North Carolina and Virginia militiamen eventually joined the American forces, which added to their logistical difficulties.

In Charleston the British general Charles, Lord Cornwallis, learned of Gates's advance and marched to Camden with a reinforcement of one thousand soldiers, doubling the size of the Camden garrison. On arrival, Cornwallis started north from Camden to intercept the enemy. The two armies bumped into each other six miles north of Camden on the night of August 15 but withdrew to await the morning. Both sides were hemmed into a narrow battlefront by the swamps near Saunder's Creek. This should have worked to the advantage of the Americans, who had numerical superiority, but in positioning his forces Gates made a fatal error. He placed all of his seasoned units on the right and the untrained militia on the left, unsupported by the Continental reserve. When the British attacked the next morning, the redcoats charged into the American left wing and routed the militiamen. Many threw down their muskets and ran without firing a shot. The British infantry wheeled left into the flank of de Kalb's Continentals. Fighting was fierce, but the Maryland and Delaware Regiments were outnumbered and soon succumbed. De Kalb fought bravely until he fell mortally wounded.

Approximately eight hundred Americans were killed or wounded, and another one thousand were taken prisoner. The army that Gates had inherited was destroyed, and he reputedly departed the battlefield with the initial British assault and rode posthaste all the way to Charlotte. The defeat at Camden was one of the worst losses suffered by the Continental army. British and Loyalist morale soared as a consequence, but Cornwallis still had to deal with bands of marauding partisans before moving into North Carolina.

By the time Cornwallis had seemingly solidified his control of South Carolina, a reformed American army was organizing in North Carolina. SAMUEL K. FORE

Lumpkin, Henry. *From Savannah to Yorktown: The American Revolution in the South.* Columbia: University of South Carolina Press, 1981.
Nelson, Paul David. *General Horatio Gates: A Biography.* Baton Rouge: Louisiana State University Press, 1976.

CAMPBELL, LORD WILLIAM (ca. 1730–1778). Governor. A younger son of John Campbell, fourth duke of Argyll, William entered the navy in 1745 and served in India. As captain of the HMS *Nightingale,* in 1763 he put into Charleston, where he met Sarah Izard, a rich heiress, then on the verge of marriage to another. But Campbell prevailed, and they were married on April 17, 1763. Returning to Britain, he successfully ran for Parliament from Argyllshire. In 1766 the Rockingham administration appointed him governor of Nova Scotia, and in June 1773 his family's influence secured his promotion to the governorship of South Carolina.

Campbell arrived in Charleston in June 1775. By then the Revolutionary Provincial Congress and its Council of Safety had usurped royal authority, and Campbell faced impossible obstacles as governor. Rumors that he was bringing arms for British-instigated Indian attacks and slave insurrections complicated his task and eventually led Revolutionary authorities to execute Thomas Jeremiah, a free black harbor pilot who was accused of being a ringleader of the impending uprising. Campbell believed him to be innocent but was powerless to intervene. The governor, however, was able to correspond with Loyalists in the backcountry. His optimistic reports of their strength contributed later to British decisions to attack South Carolina in 1776 and 1780. After Revolutionary leaders discovered Campbell's clandestine activities, he fled from Charleston on September 15, 1775. The departure of South Carolina's last royal governor enabled Revolutionary leaders to claim that George III, like King James II during the Glorious Revolution, had "abdicated the government," and accordingly, "WE OWE NO OBEDIENCE TO HIM."

During the British naval attack on Sullivan's Island in June 1776, Campbell commanded cannons aboard the HMS *Bristol* and received wounds from which he never completely recovered. Two years later he died at Southampton, England, during the first week of September 1778. ROBERT M. WEIR

Olwell, Robert. *Masters, Slaves, and Subjects: The Culture of Power in the South Carolina Low Country, 1740–1790.* Ithaca, N.Y.: Cornell University Press, 1998.

Weir, Robert M. *Colonial South Carolina: A History.* 1983. Reprint, Columbia: University of South Carolina Press, 1997.

CAROLINA BLACK CORPS. During the latter years of the Revolutionary War in South Carolina, British commanders used African American slaves, freemen, and refugees in a variety of military capacities. Although employed primarily as laborers, black Carolinians occasionally were armed by the British and used in combat. In the spring of 1782, the British formed a group of about one hundred black men into a cavalry detachment, which was used for patrol duty but also saw combat. During the final stages of Nathanael Greene's Southern Campaign, he reported that the British had as many as seven hundred black men under arms in South Carolina.

With the evacuation of Charleston pending in late 1782, British commanders pondered the fate of black soldiers under their command. A need for a black pioneer corps on the West Indian island of St. Lucia encouraged British commander Guy Carleton to order that those slaves promised freedom by the British be purchased from their owners and that volunteers from among them be enlisted for service in the West Indies at a pay rate of 8d per day. In December 1782 some 264 African American troops from South Carolina, under the command of Captain William Mackrill, arrived at St. Lucia, where they were organized into the Carolina Corps, or Carolina Black Corps. The unit served on St. Lucia until the end of the war, when it was transferred to the island of Grenada.

With the end of the war, the Carolina Black Corps continued as a provincial unit paid and supplied by the British government. It was the first black regiment to become a permanent part of the West Indian peacetime defense establishment. Although the regiment was used mainly for labor and fatigue duties, at least one company of the Carolina Black Corps was organized as dragoons (cavalry) and used to track maroons and other rebel slaves in the Caribbean. After some fifteen years of service, surviving elements of the Carolina Black Corps were enlisted into the First West India Regiment in 1798. CHARLES W. TOTH

Quarles, Benjamin. *The Negro in the American Revolution.* 1961. Reprint, Chapel Hill: University of North Carolina Press, 1996.
Tyson, George F. "The Carolina Black Corps: Legacy of Revolution (1782–1798)." *Revista/Review Interamericana* 5 (winter 1975/1976): 648–64.

CHARLESTON, SIEGE OF (April–May 1780). The siege of Charleston marked the commencement of major British operations in the South during the

British artillery emplacements in the foreground, with Charleston
harbor and city in the background. (Siege of Charleston, 1780.
Anne S.K. Brown Military Collection, Brown University)

Revolutionary War. Although they threatened Sullivan's Island in 1776 and
secured Georgia in 1779, British efforts against the rebellious southern
colonies were limited prior to 1780. General Sir Henry Clinton and Admiral
Marriot Arbuthnot led a force from New York in December 1779 to attack
Charleston. More than ten thousand British soldiers and sailors eventually
served in the campaign. Major General Benjamin Lincoln held Charleston
with six thousand men. The British landed on Seabrook Island on February
11–12, 1780, marched across Johns and James Islands, moved up the Ashley
River, and crossed at Drayton Hall on March 29.

On April 1, British working parties began the first siege parallel. The
American fortifications stretched across Charleston Neck between the Ashley and Cooper Rivers the focal point was a tabby horn-work, a remnant of
which remains in Marion Square. On April 8, British warships forced their
way past Fort Moultrie, which gave them control of Charleston harbor. Two
days later Clinton and Arbuthnot summoned the garrison, offering them the
chance to surrender; General Lincoln responded that "duty and inclination"

dictated that he defend the city "to the last extremity." The British commenced bombarding Charleston from their siege-works on April 13, and the two sides exchanged artillery and small arms fire from then until the end of the siege. The besiegers advanced toward Charleston using approach trenches and completed a second parallel on April 17.

Informed by his officers that their fortifications were too weak to hold and provisions were running low, Lincoln called a council of war to discuss their options. Some officers, including Brigadier Generals Lachlan McIntosh and William Moultrie, favored evacuating the army, but civilian officials, led by Lieutenant Governor Christopher Gadsden and Thomas Ferguson of the Privy Council, strongly discouraged the attempt. Ferguson even threatened to turn the civilians of Charleston against them. Ultimately, Lincoln and his officers offered terms of capitulation that would give the British the city and allow the American army to retreat to the backcountry. Clinton and Arbuthnot adamantly refused these proposals.

The British, meanwhile, endeavored to surround Charleston. On April 14 a force under Banastre Tarleton smashed the American cavalry posted near Moncks Corner, giving the British access to the region east of the Cooper. Clinton sent Lord Cornwallis and a detachment of troops over the Cooper to block American escape attempts. When the Americans evacuated Lempriere's Point (Hobcaw) and the Royal Navy captured Fort Moultrie, the British effectively enveloped Charleston. The completion of their third parallel allowed them to hammer the city from even closer distance. The city surrendered to the British on May 12, 1780. General Clinton disallowed the honors of war for the rebel army, meaning that they filed out of the city with colors cased and with their drummers forbidden to play a British march. The capture of Lincoln's army at Charleston was the worst American defeat of the Revolutionary War. The British victory gave them a foothold from which to begin their conquest of the southern states, an effort that eventually failed. In that sense, the triumph against Charleston was the beginning of the end for the British in America. CARL BORICK

Clinton, Henry. *The American Rebellion: Sir Henry Clinton's Narrative of His Campaigns, 1775–1782, with an Appendix of Original Documents.* Edited by William B. Willcox. New Haven, Conn.: Yale University Press, 1954.

Moultrie, William. *Memoirs of the American Revolution.* 1802. Reprint, New York: New York Times, 1968.

Uhlendorf, Bernhard A., ed. *The Siege of Charleston, with an Account of the Province of South Carolina: Diaries and Letters of Hessian Officers from the von Jungkenn Papers in the William L. Clements Library.* Ann Arbor: University of Michigan Press, 1938.

Ward, Christopher. *The War of the Revolution.* 2 vols. New York: Macmillan, 1952.

CHEROKEE WAR (1776). The Cherokee War of 1776 was an early episode in the Revolutionary War. In the summer of 1775 John Stuart, British superintendent of Indian affairs for the southern district, left his home in Charleston and moved to Florida. From there he worked to preserve the allegiance to Great Britain of the Cherokees and other Native American tribes. Stuart's assistant superintendent, Alexander Cameron, established a base of operations among the Cherokees and directed their actions against the Whigs. Combined with backcountry Loyalists, the Indians would prove a formidable force to be used against the rebels.

The Cherokees were the most powerful tribe in the region and the first to take action. The start of the Cherokee War dates from July 1, 1776, when the Cherokees struck along the western frontier. Isolated farmsteads in Ninety Six and Spartan Districts were overrun and the inhabitants killed. The backcountry militia leaders Andrew Williamson, Francis Salvador, and Andrew Pickens gathered their units and marched against the Cherokees. At Lyndley's Fort on July 15, settlers near the Saluda River were besieged by the Cherokees and Loyalists. The attackers were driven off and several men captured. On examination they were discovered to be white men dressed and painted in Cherokee fashion.

Under directions from Charleston, Williamson and other Upcountry militia captains undertook a campaign to destroy Cherokee resistance. Whig militia traveled from town to town destroying buildings and crops and dispersing the populations. By the end of the summer, Cherokee resistance was broken and the British plan to direct Indian allies against the Whigs was defeated.

The summer campaign produced two notable engagements. On August 1, 1776, a combined Loyalist and Cherokee force, led by Alexander Cameron, ambushed Andrew Williamson at Esseneca Ford, also called Seneca Old Town. Williamson's command of 330 faced as many as 1,200 Cherokees and Loyalists, who hid behind palisades. Initially driven back, the Whigs lost one of their leaders, Captain Francis Salvador of Ninety Six. Lieutenant Colonel Leroy Hammond and a troop of horsemen counterattacked and held off the Cherokees long enough for Williamson to regroup. The timely arrival of Andrew Pickens with reinforcements turned the tide of battle. Cameron and his force retreated but were pursued by the Whigs, who burned every Cherokee village and field they discovered.

About two weeks after the Esseneca battle, Williamson was made a colonel of militia and given command of a combined force of Georgians and

South Carolinians. His command systematically destroyed the lower towns of the Cherokees. On August 12 Andrew Pickens and twenty-five men were ambushed by the Cherokees at Tamassee, in present-day Oconee County. As the Cherokees emerged from the woods, Pickens ordered his men to form a defensive circle. Hand-to-hand fighting and high casualties on both sides marked the "Ring Fight" as the most desperate of the war. Pickens lost eleven men, and the Cherokees suffered sixty-five killed and fourteen wounded warriors left behind.

By the fall of 1776 the major campaign of the war had concluded. The Cherokees lost as many as two thousand killed and, despite continued British support, could fight no longer. The following spring a Cherokee delegation led by Attakulla Kulla met with officials from North and South Carolina, Georgia, and Virginia at Dewitt's Corner, in Ninety Six District. They signed a treaty on May 20, 1777, that included a cease-fire and a cession of much of the Cherokee lands within present-day Anderson, Oconee, and Pickens Counties. A few Cherokees refused to recognize the treaty. They continued raids along the Carolina-Indian border until the conclusion of the Revolutionary War. ALEXANDER MOORE

Gordon, John W. *South Carolina and the American Revolution: A Battlefield History.* Columbia: University of South Carolina Press, 2003.
Hatley, M. Thomas. *The Dividing Paths: Cherokees and South Carolinians through the Era of Revolution.* New York: Oxford University Press, 1993.
Lumpkin, Henry. *From Savannah to Yorktown: The American Revolution in the South.* Columbia: University of South Carolina Press, 1981.

COMMONS HOUSE OF ASSEMBLY (1670–1776). The dominant political institution in colonial South Carolina was the Commons House of Assembly (changed simply to "the Assembly" in 1744). It served as the lower house of the provincial legislature and was the only popularly elected branch of government in the colony. The chief theme in the early history of the Commons House was its transformation from an impotent institution to an imperious political body that jealously guarded its immense authority. Under the Fundamental Constitutions, elected representatives of the people sat together with the nobility and Lords Proprietors in a unicameral assembly (called parliaments). They had the power only to ratify or reject the statutes proposed by the Grand Council. Not until 1692 did the proprietors, responding to increasing complaints by the delegates about their lack of power, allow them to sit as a separate house, to initiate legislation, and to approve tax measures.

Over the next half-century the assemblymen, seeking to make the lower house a mirror image of the English House of Commons, usurped enormous political power from the royal governor and council. By the mid-1700s the Assembly had assumed ironclad control over all aspects of government: initiating laws, appointing revenue officers, establishing courts, supervising the Indian trade, selecting the colonial agent in London, auditing and reviewing all accounts of public officers, overseeing elections, and administering all governmental expenditures. However, the Assembly was not content with just dominating provincial affairs. It intentionally retarded the development of local government by refusing to delegate broad taxing powers to local governmental institutions. Instead, the Assembly appointed commissioners to spend the money it granted and to carry out the minutest details of local administration. In short, the Commons House of Assembly reigned supreme in South Carolina.

The Assembly's wide use of commissions and its strict control of the expenditures of local government helped to make it the hardest-working legislative body in the American colonies. Moreover, the election law of 1721 required the Commons House of Assembly to meet at least once every six months, usually in the winter and fall when planters were in Charleston for pleasure or business. With sessions lasting several months, coupled with emergency sessions called by the governor, it was not uncommon for the Assembly to sit eight months of the year. No other colonial assembly endured such long sessions. When in session, the Commons House usually met six days a week for at least six hours a day.

The long legislative sessions of the Commons House, along with the fact that members served without pay, effectively prevented all but the wealthiest and most civic-spirited men from serving in that body. Under the Fundamental Constitutions, however, any twenty-one-year-old man with five hundred acres of land could serve in the Commons House of Assembly. Under the king, aspiring assemblymen had to own at least five hundred acres and ten slaves (twenty after 1745) or £1,000 in chattels. Perhaps half the colony's adult white males met these qualifications for Commons House service. Still, voters, motivated by a negative view of human nature and a desire to control man's irrational side, elected to the Commons House economically independent (that is, very wealthy), virtuous, and able men. This shared common political ideology (often referred to as "country ideology"), combined with the colony's unrivaled economic prosperity, the constant threat of a slave rebellion, possible attack by the French and Spanish, the common economic interests between planters and merchants, and extensive intermarriage among them, encouraged a remarkable degree of political harmony to prevail in the Commons House. The lack of political discord, along with capable members committed to voluntary public service, enabled the assembly to effectively administer provincial affairs to the general satisfaction of its constituents. One glaring exception was the enormous dissatisfaction among the numerous backcountry residents who lacked representation in the Assembly until late in the colonial period. Still, the Commons House of Assembly, with its immense authority, relative independence, and general competence, provided an important legacy that later enabled the revolutionary Provincial Congress and the state General Assembly (the linear heirs of the Commons House) to effectively govern South Carolina during the turbulent decades of the late eighteenth century. KEITH KRAWCZYNSKI

Edgar, Walter, and N. Louise Bailey, eds. *Biographical Directory of the South Carolina House of Representatives*. Vol. 2, *The Commons House of Assembly, 1692–1775*. Columbia: University of South Carolina Press, 1977.

Knepper, David M. "The Political Structure of Colonial South Carolina, 1743–1776." Ph.D. diss., University of Virginia, 1971.

Sirmans, M. Eugene. *Colonial South Carolina: A Political History, 1663–1763*. Chapel Hill: University of North Carolina Press, 1966.

Weir, Robert M. *Colonial South Carolina: A History*. 1983. Reprint, Columbia: University of South Carolina Press, 1997.

Whitney, Edson L. *Government of the Colony of South Carolina*. 1895. Reprint, New York: Negro Universities Press, 1969.

CONTINENTAL REGIMENTS. In the aftermath of the battles at Lexington and Concord, the Continental Congress passed resolutions that created the Continental army in June 1775. Accordingly, a committee addressed the need for maintaining a regular army, and Congress began the task of apportioning quotas to the states. On November 4, 1775, Congress resolved to maintain "at the continental expense" three battalions for the defense of South Carolina. Continental regiments were units authorized for use by the Continental Congress and were distinct from state militia forces.

The First Provincial Congress of South Carolina raised two regiments of infantry to protect the Lowcountry against the British and a third to protect the backcountry from potential Indian raids during the summer of 1775. The first two regiments, designated the First and Second State Regiments, were adopted by the Continental Congress as the First and Second South Carolina Regiments on September 20, 1776, retroactively dated November 4,

1775. The third unit, designated as a regiment of mounted riflemen, was also adopted retroactively into the Continental Line on November 12, 1775, and designated the Third South Carolina Regiment of Rangers.

The Second Provincial Congress of South Carolina authorized a fourth regiment, an artillery unit, on November 13, 1775, and two additional infantry regiments in late February 1776. Composed of three Charleston artillery companies, the Fourth South Carolina Regiment (Artillery) was placed on the Continental Establishment on June 18, 1776, and in October two independent artillery companies from Georgetown and Beaufort were added to its ranks. The Fifth and Sixth South Carolina Regiments, deemed Rifle Regiments, were adopted into the Continental Line on March 25, 1776.

Detachments from all South Carolina Continental Regiments participated in campaigns in South Carolina, Georgia, and Florida from the "Snow Campaign" in 1775 to the Siege of Charleston in the spring of 1780. The Second Regiment successfully defended against a naval bombardment while the Third Regiment prevented an amphibious assault on the eastern end of Sullivan's Island on June 28, 1776. Additionally, all six units participated in the disastrous allied siege of Savannah in October 1779. With the exception of the Fifth and Sixth Regiments, which were consolidated with the First and Second Regiments in February 1780, all regiments of the South Carolina Continental Line were part of the American force that surrendered Charleston on May 12, 1780. Prominent members of the South Carolina Continental Line included Christopher Gadsden, William Moultrie, Francis Marion, Richard Richardson, and William Jasper. SAMUEL K. FORE

Regiment Commander(s)
First S.C. Regiment
Col. Christopher Gadsden (June 17, 1775–Sept. 16, 1776)
Col. Charles Pinckney (Sept. 16, 1776–1780)
Second S.C. Regiment
Col. William Moultrie (June 17, 1775–Sept. 16, 1776)
Col. Isaac Motte (Sept. 16, 1776–1780)
Third S.C. Regiment (Mounted Rangers)
Lt. Col. William Thomson (June 17, 1775–1780)
Fourth S.C. Regiment (Artillery)
Lt. Col. Owen Roberts (Sept. 16, 1776–June 20, 1779)
Col. Barnard Beekman (June 20, 1779–1780)
Fifth S.C. Regiment (First S.C. Rifles)
Col. Isaac Huger (Sept. 17, 1776–Jan. 9, 1777)
Lt. Col. Alexander McIntosh (Jan. 1777–1780)
Sixth S.C. Regiment (Second S.C. Rifles)
Lt. Col. Thomas Sumter (Sept. 20, 1776–1780)

Berg, Fred Anderson. *Encyclopedia of Continental Army Units: Battalions, Regiments and Independent Corps.* Harrisburg, Pa.: Stackpole, 1972.

Erd, Darby, and Fitzhugh McMaster. "The First and Second South Carolina Regiments, 1775–1780." *Military Collector & Historian* 29 (summer 1977): 70–73.

———. "The Third South Carolina Regiment (Rangers), 1775–1780." *Military Collector & Historian* 32 (summer 1980): 72–73.

Risley, Clyde A., and Fitzhugh McMaster. "Fourth South Carolina Regiment (Artillery), 1775–1780." *Military Collector & Historian* 31 (fall 1979): 124–25.

Salley, Alexander S., comp. *Records of the Regiments of the South Carolina Line in the Revolutionary War.* Baltimore: Genealogical Publishing, 1977.

Wright, Robert K. *The Continental Army.* Washington, D.C.: U.S. Army Center for Military History, 1984.

COUNCIL OF SAFETY. Prompted by rumors of British-sponsored slave and Indian attacks and news of the hostilities between British and patriot forces at Lexington and Concord, the Provincial Congress of South Carolina met for an emergency session in early June 1775. Congressional delegates hastened to cope with the rapidly deteriorating situation and began to prepare to defend the state. The congress also called for the election of a new assembly to meet later in the year. For the interim, however, it created a powerful thirteen-member committee to act as the supreme executive power in the province and to be called the Council of Safety. All thirteen members were elected to the council by ballot on the evening of June 14, 1775, including Henry Laurens, who was designated to serve as the council's president. Peter Timothy, the secretary for the Provincial Congress, would serve as secretary.

Regarding public affairs so urgent, the council held its first meeting only two days after its creation. Chief among the business of the council was the command and administration of the provincial military force and issuing paper currency to finance military expenses. Once the threat of a slave revolt in the Lowcountry had subsided, the council turned its attention to the backcountry. In addition to the Indian problem, a strong Loyalist presence began to emerge there. In an attempt to convert the disaffected, the council sent one of its most fervent members, William Henry Drayton, and two like-minded clergymen, William Tennent and Oliver Hart, on a mission into the interior of the state. But the results were disappointing. By mid-November fighting had broken out between patriots and Tories, and the council directed military operations through year's end.

When the Provincial Congress met again in November, it elected a new Council of Safety on November 16, 1775. Three new members replaced three members who had resigned, while the rest retained their seats, including

Henry Laurens as president. The new council first met on November 30, 1775, and constituted the executive power of the province until the adoption of a permanent government in March 1776. SAMUEL K. FORE

Chesnutt, David R., et al., eds. *Papers of Henry Laurens.* Vol. 10, *Dec. 12, 1774–Jan. 4, 1776.* Columbia: University of South Carolina Press, 1985.
———. *Papers of Henry Laurens.* Vol. 11, *Jan. 5, 1776–Nov. 1, 1777.* Columbia: University of South Carolina Press, 1988.
"Journal of the Council of Safety, for the Province of South Carolina, 1775." In *Collections of the South Carolina Historical Society.* Vol. 2. Charleston: South Carolina Historical Society, 1858.
"Journal of the Second Council of Safety, Appointed by the Provisional Congress, November, 1775." In *Collections of the South Carolina Historical Society.* Vol. 3. Charleston: South Carolina Historical Society, 1859.
Krawczynski, Keith. *William Henry Drayton: South Carolina Revolutionary Patriot.* Baton Rouge: Louisiana State University Press, 2001.

COWPENS, BATTLE OF (January 17, 1781). In mid-December 1780 General Daniel Morgan positioned his "Flying Army" on the Pacolet River to threaten the British stronghold of Ninety Six. British general Lord Cornwallis responded by dispatching Lieutenant Colonel Banastre Tarleton to protect Ninety Six and drive Morgan from South Carolina. Learning that Ninety Six was safe, Tarleton moved against Morgan with 1,250 men.

Morgan withdrew and assembled his force on January 16, 1781, at Hannah's Cowpens, a well-known local site situated near the North Carolina border in present-day Cherokee County. When the British reached the battlefield about daybreak on January 17, Morgan, reinforced by militia to about two thousand men, was ready to fight. He deployed more than three hundred North Carolina, South Carolina, and Georgia riflemen skirmishers, which forced Tarleton to deploy. Behind these skirmishers, Colonel Andrew Pickens led one thousand militiamen from the South Carolina Upcountry, placing them on the reverse slope and hiding many from British scouts. A third line of Delaware, Maryland, and Virginia Continentals, Virginia State Troops, and militia was to their rear, arranged so as to allow a militia withdrawal without disrupting their ranks. Continental cavalry and militia waited for an opportunity to strike.

British infantry advanced and drove back the skirmishers. Other British infantry deployed and went forward, their flanks covered by dragoons. When the British closed within thirty yards, militia fired at least five battalion volleys. Despite losses, the British charged with bayonets, routing the militia. From this point three separate lines of advance occurred. The British infantry reformed and moved within thirty yards of the Continentals, engaging them in a firefight, and British dragoons advanced on both flanks. On the American left, British dragoons scattered reforming militia. The British, in turn, were repulsed by William Washington's cavalry. On the American right, British Legion dragoons and the Seventy-first Scottish Highlanders advanced, driving off North Carolina skirmishers and then taking position beyond the American right flank. These British dragoons also were repulsed by Washington's cavalry, who charged through them, turned, and charged back.

Outflanked, the American third line commander, John Eager Howard, ordered a right company to turn and oppose the Highlanders. For several reasons the maneuver failed, and a withdrawal commenced with the Highlanders in hot pursuit. One hundred yards upfield, the Americans, who reloaded as they withdrew, turned and fired, so shocking the Highlanders that many collapsed while others ran. They were pursued by American infantry and dragoons who swept the battlefield. Tarleton's infantrymen were virtually all captured, but most British dragoons escaped. Total British casualties were about 800. American casualties were approximately 25 killed and 124 wounded.

The Battle of Cowpens was a turning point in the Revolutionary War. To recapture the prisoners, Cornwallis lightened his army and pursued Morgan and then Greene across North Carolina. This "Race to the Dan" wore out the British. They did win a costly victory at Guilford Courthouse (March 15, 1781), then marched to the coast and on to Virginia, where Cornwallis surrendered to a combined Franco-American army at Yorktown (October 19, 1781). After Guilford Courthouse, Greene returned to South Carolina and defeated British forces in a "War of Posts" during the summer of 1781. Greene's support of partisans, especially Francis Marion and Andrew Pickens, drove the British to the coast by October 1781, effectively ending British domination of interior South Carolina. LAWRENCE E. BABITS

Babits, Lawrence E. *A Devil of a Whipping: The Battle of Cowpens*. Chapel Hill: University of North Carolina Press, 1998.

Fleming, Thomas J. *Cowpens: "Downright Fighting": The Story of Cowpens*. Washington, D.C.: National Park Service, 1988.

Moncure, John. *The Cowpens Staff Ride and Battlefield Tour*. Fort Leavenworth, Kans.: Combat Studies Institute, 1966.

CUNNINGHAM, WILLIAM (?–1787). Soldier. By the end of the Revolutionary War, the Tory partisan William Cunningham had gained an unenviable reputation in South Carolina and the epithet "Bloody Bill." A cousin of the Upcountry Loyalist brothers Robert and Patrick Cunningham, William first appeared in South Carolina in the 1760s. At the outset of the Revolution, Cunningham sided with the patriots and served in the militia force that marched on the frontier post of Fort Charlotte in 1775 and in the Cherokee expedition of 1776. According to legend, Cunningham developed a relentless animosity for all patriots in 1778 after the murder of his invalid brother by backcountry Whigs.

When the British gained control of South Carolina in mid-1780, Cunningham enlisted in the provincial militia forces under the British major Patrick Ferguson. After the evacuation of Ninety Six by the British the following summer, Cunningham mustered a company of some forty men and, from a base camp in the Blue Ridge Mountains, led them on forays into the South Carolina backcountry. Rewarded with a promotion to major, Cunningham filled the ranks of his unit to some three hundred strong and set out in late autumn 1781 on an expedition that would become known as the "Bloody Scout."

Advancing to the Upcountry from Charleston, Cunningham's main force overtook and attacked a small party of thirty militia under the command of Captain Sterling Turner at Cloud's Creek on November 17, 1781. Cunningham ordered that no quarter be given after learning that Turner's force was responsible for the death of a Tory captain. After defeating Turner, Cunningham pressed on to attack a small post commanded by Colonel Joseph Hayes on the Little River only two days later. Hayes, with a handful of defenders, offered a stubborn resistance but was eventually forced to surrender. Cunningham apprehended Hayes, who reportedly still possessed a proposal of humane treatment from Cunningham in his hand, and hanged him and his executive officer. When the pole they were using as gallows broke, the Loyalists were said to have hacked Hayes and Williams to death with swords and then to have killed twelve more of the prisoners.

Cunningham began a retreat toward Charleston after learning that elements of militia forces led by Andrew Pickens and Thomas Sumter were converging on him. Retreating into the swamps near Orangeburg, Cunningham managed to elude the patriots and return to Charleston. He continued to lead raids into the South Carolina interior throughout 1782 but fled to the safety of East Florida shortly before the British evacuated Charleston in December. Still, reports of "Bloody Bill" leading incursions continued to circulate, and in 1783 the General Assembly enacted legislation intended to capture him and other "notorious offenders who disturb the peace." Spanish authorities expelled Cunningham from East Florida in 1785, claiming that he was involved in looting along the St. Mary's River. He died in Nassau, Bahamas, on January 18, 1787. SAMUEL K. FORE

Lambert, Robert Stansbury. *South Carolina Loyalists in the American Revolution.* Columbia: University of South Carolina Press, 1987.

Lumpkin, Henry. *From Savannah to Yorktown: The American Revolution in the South.* Columbia: University of South Carolina Press, 1981.

Siebert, Wilbur H. *Loyalists in East Florida, 1774 to 1785: The Most Important Documents Pertaining Thereto, Edited with an Accompanying Narrative.* 2 vols. DeLand: Florida State Historical Society, 1929.

DAVIE, WILLIAM RICHARDSON (1756–1820). Soldier, jurist, statesman. Davie was born on June 22, 1756, in Egremont Parish, Cumberlandshire, England, the eldest child of Archibald Davie and Mary Richardson. In 1764 he immigrated with his family to America, where he was raised by his uncle, the Reverend William Richardson, minister of the Waxhaw Presbyterian Church. From his uncle he received his early education, and he was enrolled in Queen's College in Charlotte, North Carolina. He entered the College of New Jersey (Princeton) in 1774 and graduated with first honors in 1776. In 1779 at the Battle of Stono, Davie was severely wounded leading a charge and barely escaped capture. It took nearly a year to recover from the wounds.

The following year, using his considerable inheritance from his uncle, Davie raised and outfitted a troop of his own. Commissioned a major, he led his men in action at the Battle of the Waxhaws (May 29, 1780), Hanging Rock (August 6, 1780), and various places in and around the Waxhaw settlement. At Hanging Rock, Davie was observed by a thirteen-year-old Andrew Jackson, the future seventh president of the United States. For the remainder of his days Jackson would consider Davie to be the beau ideal of a soldier. Davie's small command, which included white settlers and Catawba Indians, was never surprised or dispersed during its existence. His talents soon caught the eye of General Nathanael Greene. He persuaded Davie to become commissary general of the Southern Army in early 1781. In this post he served admirably, being able to feed the army even though the land in both Carolinas had been devastated by war. After the war ended, Davie settled in Halifax, North Carolina. He married Sarah Jones on April 11, 1782, and they were the parents of six children. Taking an active role in North Carolina politics, he served in the North Carolina House of Commons from 1784 until 1798, when he was elected governor. He favored a lenient policy toward Loyalists and was the leading figure in the establishment of the University of

North Carolina in 1789. In 1787 Davie was a delegate to the Constitutional Convention in Philadelphia. A lifelong Federalist, he approved of the Constitution and campaigned vigorously for its passage. In 1799 President John Adams appointed Davie as one of three delegates to negotiate agreements on amity and commerce with France.

Davie returned to South Carolina in late 1805, retiring to his Tivoli plantation in Lancaster District. An active member of the South Carolina Agricultural Society, Davie also assisted in negotiating the boundary dispute between North and South Carolina. In 1812 he was nominated for vice president on the Federalist ticket and was briefly considered for command of the U.S. Army during the War of 1812. His last public office was as a commissioner of the Board of Public Works in South Carolina. Davie died on November 5, 1820, and was buried at Old Waxhaw Presbyterian Church in Lancaster. RHETT A. ADAMS

Robinson, Blackwell. *William R. Davie.* Chapel Hill: University of North Carolina Press, 1957.

DE KALB, JOHANN (1721–1780). Soldier. The man who was to be known in America as "Baron de Kalb" was born Johann Kalb to peasant parents in the Bavarian hamlet of Hüttendorf, Germany, on June 19, 1721. He began his military service in 1743 as a lieutenant in a French army regiment under the name of Jean de Kalb. His military career in Europe culminated in 1776, when he was commissioned a brigadier general in the French army. De Kalb subsequently decided to seek his military fortune in America, where he was contracted as a major general in the Continental army. Along with the young Marquis de Lafayette, de Kalb sailed for the colonies in April 1777 and arrived off the coast of Georgetown, South Carolina, in June.

After three years of service with the Continental army, de Kalb received an assignment equivalent with his rank. On April 3, 1780, he was ordered to the relief of Charleston, South Carolina, at the head of the Maryland and Delaware Continental regiments. On July 25, 1780, de Kalb surrendered command to Major General Horatio Gates at Deep River, North Carolina, but remained with the army at the head of his division. Gates chose to directly attack the British garrison at Camden. Three weeks later, on August 16, Gates met Lord Cornwallis six miles north of Camden near Saunder's Creek. Shortly after the action began, the American militia broke and fled in disorder. The Continentals under de Kalb stood firm and were almost annihilated. De Kalb fell with several wounds and died three days later, on August 19, 1780, a prisoner of war. He was buried by his captors with military honors.

In 1825 Lafayette, his comrade in arms, laid the cornerstone of a monument to de Kalb in Camden. SAMUEL K. FORE

Kapp, Friedrich. *Life of John Kalb.* New York: Holt, 1884.
Sifton, Paul G., ed. "La Caroline Méridionale: Some French Sources of South Carolina Revolutionary History, with Two Unpublished Letters of Baron de Kalb." *South Carolina Historical Magazine* 66 (April 1965): 102–8.
Zucker, A. E. *General de Kalb, Lafayette's Mentor.* Chapel Hill: University of North Carolina Press, 1966.

DRAYTON, WILLIAM HENRY (1742–1779). Revolutionary leader, planter. Drayton was born in September 1742 at Drayton Hall in St. Andrew's Parish, the son of John Drayton, a wealthy planter and member of the Provincial Council, and Charlotta Bull, daughter of Lieutenant Governor William Bull. At the age of ten William Henry went to England to complete his education, but he returned home at the behest of his father in 1763 before he could finish his degree at Balliol College, Oxford. A year later Drayton married Dorothy Golightly, one of the wealthiest heiresses in the colony. Their union produced four children, of whom only Mary and John survived childhood.

Financially secure and politically well connected, William Henry sought public office. He won a seat in the South Carolina Assembly in 1765 but lost it in the following election because of indifferent service. Nevertheless, Drayton found himself at the center of political affairs. In July 1769 he wrote a polemic in the *South-Carolina Gazette* opposing the popular extralegal nonimportation association (established in defiance to the recently enacted Townshend Duties) as "*a base, illegal decree*" designed to "*ruin* and *overthrow* our *happy constitution.*" The letter started a caustic five-month public debate with nonimportation leaders that changed few minds and resulted in Drayton's being ostracized politically, socially, and economically in South Carolina. In January 1770 he sailed for England, where he hoped his views would find greater acceptance.

In England, Drayton was introduced at court as a supporter of the crown's prerogative. To further display his loyalty, Drayton published in 1771 *The Letters of Freeman,* a compilation of his newspaper articles on the nonimportation debate. His allegiance earned him a position on the Royal Council in Charleston. However, Drayton's aspiration for additional posts was frustrated when the Ministry appointed Englishmen to numerous offices that Drayton sought for himself. Increasing his frustration was Parliament's passage in 1774 of the Coercive Acts, measures which convinced Drayton that the "liberty and property of the American [were] at the pleasure of a despotic power." In August of that year Drayton vented his personal and intellectual frustration with the crown and Parliament in *A Letter from Freeman,* a pamphlet addressed to the First Continental Congress in which he outlined American rights and proposed a blueprint for the reform of the British Empire that denied Parliament's jurisdiction over the colonies. Drayton further antagonized crown officers both in London and in Charleston when on his tour of the circuit courts in November 1774 he urged grand jurymen to select "freedom over slavery" and defy British authority. Drayton's *Freeman* essay and judicial charges prompted a disappointed William Bull to suspend his nephew from the Royal Council in early 1775.

However, Drayton's outspoken views made him one of the most popular Whigs in the colony. He won a seat in the Provincial Congress in January 1775 and soon after sat on all important revolutionary committees. Drayton used his extensive powers to lead raids against the city's royal post office and armories, thereby obtaining both crucial information regarding the intentions of the British Ministry and arms for the patriot forces. During the summer of 1775, Drayton led a five-man commission on a six-week tour of the backcountry to suppress the large number of Loyalists in the region. In the face of great odds, Drayton managed to procure a treaty of neutrality from Loyalist leaders at a conference in the town of Ninety Six.

Whig leaders in Charleston rewarded Drayton for his achievement by electing him president of the Provincial Congress. In this role he encouraged the creation of a navy, raising and training troops and erecting fortifications. Speaking to the Provincial Congress on February 6, 1776, Drayton became the first prominent Carolinian to openly call for the establishment of a new government and separation from Great Britain. The next month that body drafted a constitution replacing the royal charter. Drayton went on to play a leading role in creating the new state constitution adopted in 1778. In January of that year Drayton also proposed numerous amendments to the recently published Articles of Confederation. Attached to his proposal was an alternative plan of confederation augmenting the power of the individual states and protecting southern interests.

Drayton's essay on America's first federal charter perhaps explains his election to the Continental Congress in 1778. A tireless worker, Drayton served on nearly ninety ad hoc and five standing committees during his seventeen months in Congress. As one of America's most effective polemicists, Drayton focused on opposing British attempts at reconciliation. His last months in Congress, however, were spent in various bitter quarrels in that politically charged body. In his spare time Drayton compiled documents for a history of the Revolution, an undertaking left unfinished when he died of typhus in Philadelphia on September 3, 1779. KEITH KRAWCZYNSKI

Dabney, William M., and Marion Dargan. *William Henry Drayton and the American Revolution.* Albuquerque: University of New Mexico Press, 1962.

Drayton, John. *Memoirs of the American Revolution as Relating to the State of South Carolina.* 2 vols. 1821. Reprint, New York: New York Times, 1969.

Gibbes, Robert W. *Documentary History of the American Revolution.* 3 vols. 1853–1857. Reprint, Spartanburg, S.C.: Reprint Company, 1972.

Krawczynski, Keith. *William Henry Drayton: South Carolina Revolutionary Patriot.* Baton Rouge: Louisiana State University Press, 2001.

EUTAW SPRINGS, BATTLE OF (September 8, 1781). The Battle of Eutaw Springs was the last major engagement in South Carolina between American and British forces during the Revolutionary War. In the bloody encounter, some two thousand Continental and militia soldiers commanded by General Nathanael Greene clashed with 2,300 British regulars and Loyalists under Lieutenant Colonel Alexander Stewart. Although Greene was forced to leave the field, the British were equally mauled and retreated to Charleston, abandoning the South Carolina Upcountry. The battle site is located in Orangeburg County near Eutawville, and a portion of the battlefield is a state historic site.

British forces were at Eutaw Springs on September 7, encamped near a sturdy two-story brick home with palisaded garden, when Greene completed the consolidation of his forces at Burdell's plantation about seven miles away. Early the following morning, Greene put his army on the march. Stewart was not aware that the Americans were so close, and he had that morning sent out foragers to collect sweet potatoes. Four miles from Eutaw Springs, the vanguard of the American army ran into the British escort protecting the rooting party. Many of the unarmed foragers were captured. Reacting quickly, Stewart sent forward additional troops to delay the Americans and formed his main army in a single line about two hundred yards west of his Eutaw Springs campgrounds. He anchored his right flank on Eutaw Creek with the brick house, occupied by a covering force, behind the line. Greene used a formation that had seen success at the Battle of Cowpens. The militiamen were placed in the front line, with the battle-hardened Continentals behind them in the second line. Advancing, the Americans pushed back the British skirmishers until they met the main body, at which point there began a bloody back-and-forth duel. Eventually the center of the American line began to buckle under the intense action, and Stewart directed an advance.

But his forces became disorderly and Greene saw his opportunity. He ordered the Continentals forward in a bayonet attack that forced the British left flank to fall back and retreat through their campsite. On the verge of a major victory, many of the American troops thought the battle won and left the fighting to loot the British camp. This action cost Greene his victory, for the British right flank had not retreated and those secure in the house began a heavy fire, which threw the Americans into confusion and allowed Stewart to rally his troops for a counterattack. Greene got control of his troops before disaster struck, and behind a covering force they retreated back to Burdell's, leaving the field and two artillery pieces to the British. Losses on both sides were high: the British admitted to 683 killed, wounded, and missing and the Americans reported 517. Among the American unit commanders were many notable patriots, including Francis Marion; Otho Williams; William Washington, who was captured; Henry Lee; Andrew Pickens, who was wounded; and Wade Hampton. STEVEN D. SMITH

McCrady, Edward. *The History of South Carolina in the Revolution.* 2 vols. New York: Macmillan, 1901–1902.

Pancake, John S. *This Destructive War: The British Campaign in the Carolinas, 1780–1782.* University: University of Alabama Press, 1985.

FAYSSOUX, PETER (ca. 1745–1795). Physician. Fayssoux was born and grew up in Charleston, the son of Daniel Fayssoux, a Huguenot émigré, and his wife Frances. In 1766 Fayssoux went to medical school in Edinburgh, where he was a classmate of Benjamin Rush. Returning to South Carolina in 1769, he found the city full of quacks: "It is Sufficient for a man to call himself a Doctor, & he immediately becomes one, & finds fools to employ him," he complained to Rush. On January 29, 1772, Fayssoux married Sarah "Sally" Wilson, who died in 1776. The following year, on March 29, 1777, Fayssoux married Ann Smith Johnston. The marriages produced thirteen children, six of whom died in infancy or early childhood.

Early in the Revolutionary War, Fayssoux attended the sick on James Island and provided advice on extracting salt from seawater. By 1778 he was serving as "senior physician" of the South Carolina branch of the Continental army, having been appointed by Dr. David Oliphant, director of the hospital. Fayssoux was with General William Moultrie at the Battle of Sullivan's Island on June 28, 1776. In 1779, when Moultrie repulsed a British force threatening Beaufort, Fayssoux was given the task of remaining with the sick until Moultrie could supply the necessary carriages to remove them. In 1780 Fayssoux was named physician and surgeon general of the Southern

Department. Captured at the fall of Charleston, he was released in order to attend to the sick and wounded in the city. After the Battle of Eutaw Springs on September 8, 1781, the responsibility for the wounded fell to Fayssoux. At the end of the war Fayssoux was treating the sick and wounded in Camden, where he stayed until March 1782.

After the war Fayssoux became a member of the Faculty of Physic in Charleston, which was the first evidence of organized medicine in South Carolina. Along with Alexander Baron and David Ramsay, Fayssoux comprised the organizing committee charged with reporting a plan to improve "the Science of Medicine . . . amongst the Practitioners in this City." He was a founding member and the first president of the Medical Society of South Carolina, which held its first meeting at Fayssoux's home on December 24, 1789. Though he made no literary contributions to medicine, his leadership in the early organization of medicine and his contributions to the Revolution placed him among the major medical figures of his time. His peers described Fayssoux as "possessed of a clear discriminating judgment" and as a skillful practitioner of "the Healing Art."

In 1786 Fayssoux was elected to the General Assembly, where he represented St. John's Berkeley Parish until 1790. He voted against ratification of the federal Constitution in 1788 but afterward accepted the new government amicably. In addition to his medical and political activities, Fayssoux was involved with the Charleston Library Society, the Charleston Museum (as a curator), the Society of the Cincinnati (founding member), and the St. Cecilia Society. He died on February 1, 1795, of apoplectic stroke and was buried in the churchyard of First (Scots) Presbyterian Church, Charleston. JANE MC-CUTCHEN BROWN

Davidson, Chalmers G. *Friend of the People: The Life of Dr. Peter Fayssoux of Charleston, South Carolina.* Columbia: Medical Association of South Carolina, 1950.
Waring, Joseph I. *History of Medicine in South Carolina.* Vol. 1, 1670–1825. Columbia: South Carolina Medical Association, 1964.

FISHING CREEK, BATTLE OF (August 18, 1780). After the Battle of Camden, Lieutenant Colonel Banastre Tarleton and his British legion pursued the patriot general Thomas Sumter and his troops in the hope of recapturing British prisoners and stores taken by Sumter in a raid just prior to the battle. After an aggressive pursuit, Tarleton's legion neared Sumter's force along the Catawba River in South Carolina. Although Sumter was aware of the British presence across the river, he continued marching up the west bank of the river throughout the morning of August 18, 1780. In the meantime, Tarleton secured boats and sent his command across the river and then continued on a forced march after the enemy.

Sumter, feeling safe in the belief that the British were far enough away on the other side of the river, halted his command to rest at noon at Fishing Creek. The march had been a hard one, under intensely hot and humid conditions and over numerous steep hills, and his men had pushed themselves hard. After posting sentries outside the camp, Sumter allowed his men to stack arms and do as they pleased. Some men napped and some swam in the river, while others lounged around getting drunk.

As Sumter's men relaxed, Tarleton's legion continued their forced march. Many were overcome with the heat, and when they insisted that they could go no further, Tarleton decided to push forward with 160 men, although the enemy force numbered nearly 800. When Tarleton reached the confines of Sumter's camp, he easily subdued the sentries and then swiftly attacked the rebels. His lightning-fast attack made it impossible for the Americans to fight back and left them no choice but to run for their lives. The Americans suffered heavy losses during the fight, including 150 men killed or wounded, 350 captured, and the loss of their British prisoners and plunder and their arms, ammunition wagons, baggage, and other stores. Tarleton's force had just 16 men killed or wounded. Coming on the heels of the humiliating defeat at Camden, the rout of Sumter's force at Fishing Creek marked the low point of the patriot cause in South Carolina. KENDRA DEBANY

Buchanan, John. *The Road to Guilford Courthouse: The American Revolution in the Carolinas.* New York: Wiley, 1997.

Morrill, Dan L. *Southern Campaigns of the American Revolution.* Baltimore: Nautical & Aviation Publishing, 1993.

Russell, David Lee. *The American Revolution in the Southern Colonies.* Jefferson, N.C.: McFarland, 2000.

FORT JOHNSON. Located on Charleston harbor, Fort Johnson was constructed on the northeast point of James Island in 1708. Named after the colony's proprietary governor Nathaniel Johnson, it was apparently built in response to the 1706 French and Spanish attack on Charleston. The original fortification was replaced by a new work in 1759, which was garrisoned under British authority during the colonial period. During the Stamp Act crisis of 1765, Fort Johnson briefly housed revenue stamps and provided protection to British stamp officials. It was occupied by South Carolina troops under the command of Isaac Motte in 1775 and remained in American hands until 1780, when advancing British troops found it destroyed. WILLIS J. KEITH

Mustard, Harry S. "On the Building of Fort Johnson." *South Carolina Historical Magazine* 64 (July 1963): 129–35.
Wilcox, Arthur M., and Warren Ripley. *The Civil War at Charleston.* Charleston, S.C.: News and Courier, 1966.

FORT MOTTE. Fort Motte was the plantation home of Rebecca Motte that was fortified by the British during the Revolutionary War. Located on a high prominence overlooking the Congaree River, the fort served as a depot for supply convoys between Charleston, Ninety Six, and Camden. The fort consisted of the Motte house surrounded by a ditch and a parapet. After the capture of Fort Watson, Brigadier General Francis Marion and Lieutenant Colonel Henry Lee moved north on May 6, 1781, and began a siege. In the fort were Lieutenant Donald McPherson with 140 British regulars plus a small detachment of dragoons. A British relief force under the command of Francis Lord Rawdon came within sight on May 11, giving hope to the besieged garrison. However, Marion and Lee, realizing that they had to act quickly, decided to set Mrs. Motte's house on fire. Lee asserted in his *Memoirs* that upon informing Mrs. Motte of their decision she offered the bow and arrows for the task, but William Dobein James, a Marion biographer, dismisses this story, stating that the fire was started by slinging burning rosin onto the roof. Either way, Mrs. Motte's home was set afire and Marion's six-pound cannon kept the British from putting it out. The British were forced to surrender. The fire was extinguished, and that evening Mrs. Motte entertained both the British and American officers. Although only two men died in the battle, several Loyalists were hanged the next day. Marion saved another. STEVEN D. SMITH

James, William Dobein. *A Sketch of the Life of Brig. Gen. Francis Marion.* 1821. Reprint, Marietta, Ga.: Continental Book Company, 1948.
Lee, Henry. *The Revolutionary War Memoirs of General Henry Lee.* 1869. Reprint, New York: Da Capo, 1998.
Rankin, Hugh F. *Francis Marion: The Swamp Fox.* New York: Crowell, 1973.

FORT MOULTRIE. This was the site of the June 28, 1776, American victory in the Revolutionary War.

Fort Moultrie was located on Sullivan's Island at the mouth of Charleston harbor. Construction began in February 1776 on the then-unnamed palmetto log and sand fort. A square fort with corner bastions, its walls were five hundred feet long, more than ten feet high, and sixteen feet apart, with the space between filled with sand. On June 28, 1776, Colonel William Moultrie commanded the half-completed fort, which mounted thirty-one

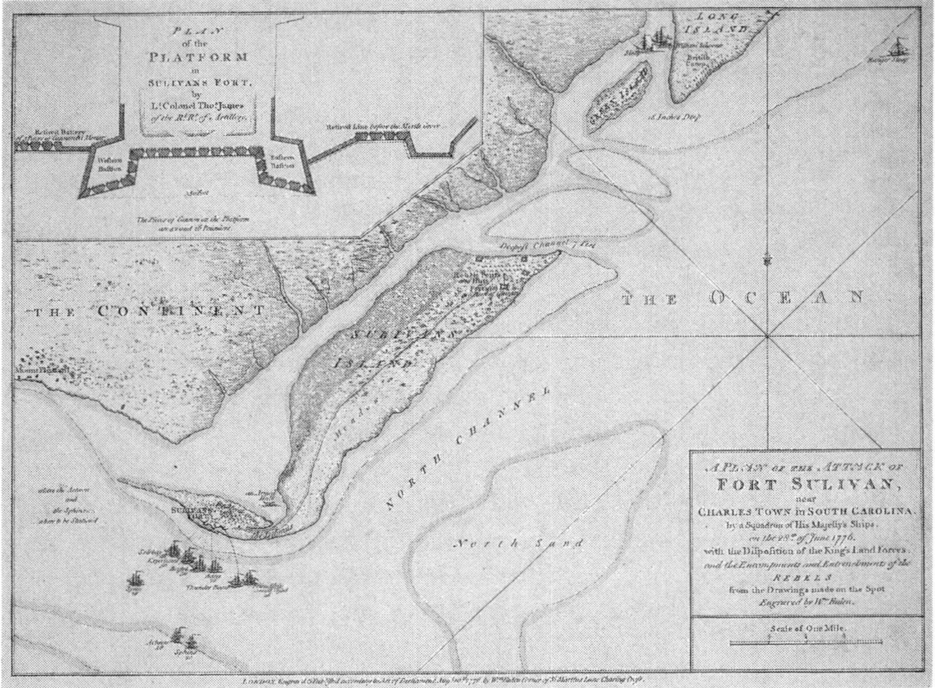

"A plan of the attack of Fort Sullivan, near Charles Town in South
Carolina, by a squadron of His Majesty's ships on 28th of June 1776."
Published 1776. Courtesy, Royal Collection Trust.

cannons and a garrison of more than four hundred soldiers. In the nine-
and-one-half-hour battle, nine British warships with almost three hundred
cannons were defeated. After the victory, the fort was completed and named
in Moultrie's honor. After the war the fort was not garrisoned and fell into
disrepair. RICHARD W. HATCHER III

Stokeley, Jim. *Fort Moultrie: Constant Defender.* Washington, D.C.: United States Department of the Interior, 1985.

FORT WATSON. Fort Watson, named for Colonel John Watson, was one of
a series of British supply depots between Charleston and Camden during
the Revolutionary War. The fort was located at Wright's Bluff overlooking
Scott's Lake and was constructed between late December 1780 and the end
of January 1781. Scott's Lake has since been inundated by Lake Marion,
and the fort site is protected by the Santee National Wildlife Refuge. The

British constructed the formidable stockaded post on top of an ancient Indian mound, surrounding it with three rows of sharpened tree trunks and branches called abatis. On April 15, 1781, the Americans under the command of Francis Marion and Henry Lee invested the fort and began a siege that lasted eight days and ended with its capture. The fort's garrison included seventy-eight regular British soldiers and thirty-six Loyalists under the command of Lieutenant James McKay. With the strong garrison, the abatis, and the cleared land around the fort, Marion and Lee realized that a frontal assault to take the fort would be too costly. At the suggestion of Major Hezekiah Maham, the Americans constructed a log tower near the fort. This allowed riflemen to fire into the fort and protected an assault party that pulled away the abatis, forcing the British to surrender. The fort was destroyed. STEVEN D. SMITH

Ferguson, Leland G. "An Archeological-Historical Analysis of Fort Watson: December 1780–April 1781." In *Research Strategies in Historical Archaeology,* edited by Stanley South. New York: Academic Press, 1977.

James, William Dobein. *A Sketch of the Life of Brig. Gen. Francis Marion.* 1821. Reprint, Marietta, Ga.: Continental Book Company, 1948.

Lee, Henry. *The Revolutionary War Memoirs of General Henry Lee.* 1869. Reprint, New York: Da Capo, 1998.

Rankin, Hugh F. *Francis Marion: The Swamp Fox.* New York: Crowell, 1973.

GADSDEN, CHRISTOPHER (1724–1805). Patriot, merchant. Gadsden was born in Charleston on February 16, 1724, the son of Elizabeth and Thomas Gadsden, a collector of customs. Gadsden received a classical education in England before completing a four-year apprenticeship to a prominent Philadelphia factor. Between 1745 and 1747 he served as purser aboard the British man-of-war *Aldborough.* With money from his seafaring service and a large inheritance from his parents, who had both died by 1741, Gadsden launched one of the most successful mercantile careers in the province. By 1774 he owned four stores, several merchant vessels, two rice plantations (worked by more than ninety slaves), a residential district called Gadsdenboro in Charleston, and one of the largest wharfs in North America.

Possessing financial independence and a civic spirit, Gadsden pursued public office. In 1757 he began his nearly three decades of service in the Commons House of Assembly. He first revealed himself as a vocal defender of American rights during the Cherokee War by attacking the British colonel James Grant for taking command of local troops above provincial Colonel Thomas Middleton. Gadsden continued to defy British authority as a member of the assembly by opposing the governor and Royal Council in their attempt to infringe on the legislature's right to raise troops, control money bills, and determine the election of its own members. Governor Thomas Boone marked Gadsden a troublemaker in 1762 and used a violation of a minor electoral practice to deny him his seat in the Commons House. The ensuing controversy between the governor and Gadsden swelled the merchant's reputation as a defender of colonial rights and helped transform him into a zealous American patriot.

Gadsden continued to champion American home rule and to oppose Parliamentary supremacy at the Stamp Act Congress in New York in 1765. During the next decade, Gadsden joined with Charleston mechanics (Sons of Liberty) to lead the local "patriot party" against every perceived infringement of America's rights by Parliament. Gadsden's influence and dedication earned him election to the First Continental Congress, where his extremism manifested itself in proposals for Congress to reject all Parliamentary legislation passed since 1763, to attack the British fleet in American waters, and to instruct each colony to prepare for war. Gadsden returned to South Carolina in February 1776 to serve as colonel of the First Regiment and as a member of the Provincial Congress, where he promoted independence and coauthored the South Carolina constitution of 1776. That summer he helped repulse the British navy's attack on Charleston, conduct that earned him a position as brigadier general in the Continental Army. Two years later Gadsden helped secure the disestablishment of the Anglican Church and popular election of senators in the state's 1778 constitution. But the conservative faction dominating the assembly managed to dampen the firebrand's influence in the new government by electing Gadsden to the impotent position of vice president (as the office of lieutenant governor was then known).

While Gadsden's zealous and suspicious personality was ideal for organizing American resistance, it was counterproductive in the post-1776 political structure. In 1777 he impulsively resigned his commission as brigadier general over a petty dispute with General Robert Howe. The following year Gadsden violently upset the masses by favoring leniency toward local Tories. And while serving as lieutenant governor in 1780, Gadsden's irrational temperament cost the United States more than two thousand Continental troops when Charleston fell to the British. Following a ten-month imprisonment in St. Augustine, Gadsden returned to South Carolina to rebuild his many business interests, which suffered considerably during the war. He returned to public service briefly in 1788 to vote for ratification of the United States Constitution and again in 1790 to serve in the state's constitutional convention.

Gadsden married three times. On July 28, 1746, he married Jane Godfrey. The couple had two children. He married Mary Hasell on December 29, 1755. His second marriage produced four children. Following Mary's death in 1768, Gadsden married Ann Wragg on April 14, 1776. They had no children. Gadsden died on August 28, 1805, from head injuries suffered in a fall near his home in Charleston. He was buried in St. Philip's Churchyard. KEITH KRAWCZYNSKI

Godbold, E. Stanley, Jr., and Robert H. Woody. *Christopher Gadsden and the American Revolution.* Knoxville: University of Tennessee Press, 1982.

McDonough, Daniel J. *Christopher Gadsden and Henry Laurens: The Parallel Lives of Two American Patriots.* Selinsgrove, Pa.: Susquehanna University Press, 2000.

Walsh, Richard. *Charleston's Sons of Liberty: A Study of the Artisans, 1763–1789.* Columbia: University of South Carolina Press, 1959.

———. "Christopher Gadsden: Radical or Conservative Revolutionary?" *South Carolina Historical Magazine* 63 (October 1962): 195–203.

———, ed. *The Writings of Christopher Gadsden, 1746–1805.* Columbia: University of South Carolina Press, 1966.

GADSDEN FLAG. Consisting of a gray, coiled rattlesnake on a bright yellow background, with the words "don't tread on me" inscribed beneath, the Gadsden flag became a popular symbol of the American Revolution. Dating back to the origins of the French and Indian War, the indigenous rattlesnake had been an important political symbol in the American colonies. In protest to British colonial policy, Benjamin Franklin designed a disconnected serpent with the ominous warning, "Join or Die," as a symbol of unity. Growing in popularity, the rattlesnake later appeared in newspapers and on colonial currency.

Inferential evidence and the weight of tradition attribute the creation of this particular flag to Christopher Gadsden, a delegate from South Carolina to the Continental Congress. Returning to Charleston from Congress, Gadsden presented "an elegant standard" to the South Carolina Provincial Congress on February 9, 1776. This flag was that day ordered preserved in the hall of the South Carolina Provincial Congress. As a member of the Naval Committee of the Continental Congress, Gadsden had also presented the flag to Esek Hopkins, commander-in-chief of the Continental Navy, who used a version of the Gadsden flag as the first navy jack. The rattlesnake and motto were later incorporated into a flag used by the naval forces of South Carolina as fitting symbols of the defensive posture of the disgruntled colonists by 1776. SAMUEL K. FORE

Godbold, E. Stanley, Jr., and Robert H. Woody. *Christopher Gadsden and the American Revolution.* Knoxville: University of Tennessee Press, 1982.

Rankin, Hugh F. "The Naval Flag of the American Revolution." *William and Mary Quarterly,* 3d ser., 11 (July 1954): 339–53.

Richardson, Edward W. *Standards and Colors of the American Revolution.* Philadelphia: University of Pennsylvania Press, 1982.

GEIGER, EMILY (ca. 1762–?). Revolutionary War heroine. Geiger was the daughter of John Geiger, a German farmer. Little is known of her early life.

In June 1781 Emily Geiger volunteered to be a courier for General Nathanael Greene, who needed an urgent message delivered to General Thomas Sumter. With the British watching the roads between Greene and Sumter, Geiger argued that a woman could go, since a woman would probably raise less British suspicion than a man. Greene consented and sent her on the mission. Geiger evaded capture the first day, but the British stopped her on the second day. While waiting for the British to bring a woman to search her, she read and memorized Greene's message and then ate it. Finding no incriminating message, the British released her. She found her way to Sumter and delivered the message she had memorized. As a result of her persistence, Sumter's forces met with other patriot forces at British-held Orangeburg to carry out Greene's plan of attack.

After the Revolutionary War, Geiger married a planter named John Threrwitz (or Threewitts). They lived near Granby, South Carolina. Geiger's date of death is unknown. She was buried in Threrwitz Cemetery in Lexington County. BRENDA THOMPSON SCHOOLFIELD

Bodie, Idella. *South Carolina Women.* Orangeburg, S.C.: Sandlapper, 1991.

Harkness, David James. "Heroines of the American Revolution." *University of Tennessee Newsletter* 60 (February 1961): 1–16.

Rhett, Claudine. "Emily Geiger: A Heroine of the Revolution." *American Monthly Magazine* 8 (March 1896): 302–304.

GILLON, ALEXANDER (1741–1794). Congressman, merchant, naval officer, legislator. Gillon was born in Rotterdam, Holland, on August 13, 1741, the son of Alexander Gillon and Mary Harris. Gillon's fluency in several languages, handsome appearance, and social graces helped him rise quickly in the commercial trade. Gillon first arrived in the American colonies as the master of the brigantine *Surprize,* docking at Philadelphia in December 1764. Within two years, Gillon met Mary Splatt Cripps, widow of William Cripps, and the two were married on July 6, 1766. The union produced one daughter. His wife died in 1787, whereupon Gillon married Ann Purcell on February 10, 1789. This marriage produced three children.

Gillon settled in Charleston in 1766, prospering in commercial ventures, operating a store and merchant vessels. In 1773 he opened the firm of Alexander Gillon & Company with his stepsons, William and John Splatt Cripps. Reorganized under Gillon and William Cripps, the firm operated a store on the bay that sold foodstuffs and wines. The lucrative venture enabled Gillon to retire from the mercantile trade in 1777, at which time he owned a house and lot on East Bay Street, a dock on the Cooper River, another fifteen lots in Charleston, and 5,500 acres of land on the Congaree River.

Gillon first came to public attention when he appeared before the Liberty Tree Committee on January 24, 1770, for violation of the Non-Importation Association boycott. Early in the Revolution, Gillon eagerly attached himself to the patriot cause. He was a member of the Committee of Ninety-Nine (1774), organized the German Fusiliers in 1775 (which he commanded until 1777), and served in the Second Provincial Congress (1775–1776). In 1776 he put his commercial abilities to use supplying munitions to the Continental Congress. In February 1778 Gillon turned down another supply contract with the Continental Congress to accept command of the South Carolina Navy with the rank of commodore. In Amsterdam, in May 1780, Gillon leased the frigate *South Carolina* from the Chevalier Luxembourg of France and set sail from Amsterdam in August 1781. After an ill-fated voyage across the Atlantic, which saw Gillon financially ruined, the *South Carolina* arrived in Philadelphia in May 1782. The *South Carolina* was captured leaving Philadelphia under command of John Joyner in December 1782. The resulting claims against the state arising out of Gillon's brief command of the *South Carolina* were not fully settled until 1856.

After the Revolution, Gillon served in the General Assembly (1783–1791), representing the city districts of St. Philip's and St. Michael's, then the backcountry district of Saxe Gotha. Gillon also became immersed in the conflict between pro-British and anti-British factions in Charleston. He helped found the Marine Anti-Britannic Society and firmly allied himself with Charleston mechanics and the antiaristocratic faction in Charleston politics. In 1784 Gillon lost the election for intendant of Charleston to Richard Hutson, after which he increasingly associated himself with his backcountry supporters and officially moved to his estate, Gillon's Retreat, in Orangeburg District. Reelected to the Tenth General Assembly, Gillon chose instead to serve in Congress (1793–1794) representing the Beaufort-Orangeburg District. He died on October 6, 1794, at Gillon's Retreat and was buried in the plantation cemetery. J. BRYAN COLLARS

Bailey, N. Louise, and Elizabeth Ivey Cooper, eds. *Biographical Directory of the South Carolina House of Representatives.* Vol. 3, *1775–1790.* Columbia: University of South Carolina Press, 1981.

Nadelhaft, Jerome J. *The Disorders of War: The Revolution in South Carolina.* Orono: University of Maine Press, 1981.

GRIMKÉ, JOHN FAUCHERAUD (1752–1819). Legislator, jurist. Grimké was born in Charleston on December 16, 1752, the son of merchant John Paul Grimké and his wife, Mary Faucheraud. After receiving his bachelor of arts degree from Trinity College, Cambridge, in 1774, Grimké returned to Charleston. His marriage to Mary Smith on October 12, 1784, produced fourteen children, including noted abolitionists Angelina and Sarah Grimké.

His judicial prominence stemmed from early political and military involvement. As a student in England in 1774, Grimké joined twenty-eight other Americans in protesting the Boston Port Bill. Shortly after returning to Charleston in September 1775, Grimké organized an artillery unit for service in the Revolutionary War. Rising to the rank of lieutenant colonel by 1779, he was captured at the fall of Charleston. He was later imprisoned by the British for allegedly violating his parole, but escaped to join General Nathanael Greene's army, where he served the remainder of the war.

In 1782 Grimké began the first of five terms representing the city parishes of St. Philip's and St. Michael's in the General Assembly, including a term as Speaker of the House from 1785 to 1786. Soon after the war, the legislature revived state law courts and named Grimké an associate justice of the Court of Common Pleas and General Sessions in March 1783. Many upstate citizens loyal to Britain during the war feared the nascent judiciary would extract revenge and lack impartiality. At his first grand jury charge in Camden in November 1783, Grimké sought to calm those concerns by declaring "We are all Americans" and that "our passions" were the only enemy of legal justice. Soon after his appointment, the legislature created county courts to hear minor cases, where laymen versed in local custom presided. To provide courtroom standards, Grimké published *The South Carolina Justice of Peace* in 1784 as a guide for officers of the new judiciary. In 1790 Grimké published the first updated digest of state laws in fifty years, *The Public Laws of the State of South Carolina.* Listing relevant and applicable laws in the period between the Revolutionary War and ratification of the Constitution, his digest provided a groundwork for judicial uniformity and the professionalization of legal study in South Carolina.

Grimké also resisted outside intimidation of the young state judiciary. In 1785 he encountered hostile debtors on his circuit in Camden. Grimké dismissed the "Camden Court House Riot" as an "illegal measure" and maintained the legitimacy of the court. As a delegate to the state constitutional convention in May 1790, Grimké introduced the provisions separating the judiciary from the legislature and requiring a two-thirds vote for judicial impeachment. In 1811 he took advantage of this proviso to defeat impeachment charges brought against him by political opponents.

During his thirty-six years on the bench, Grimké helped establish fundamental principles of South Carolina jurisprudence by advocating professionalization of legal study, uniformity of law, and judicial independence. After an extended illness, Grimké died in Long Branch, New Jersey, on August 9, 1819. ELI A. POLIAKOFF

King, Stephen Earl. "The Honorable John Faucheraud Grimké of South Carolina." Master's thesis, University of South Carolina, 1993.

GUERARD, BENJAMIN (?–1788). Governor. Benjamin Guerard, the son of John Guerard and Elizabeth Hill, was baptized in Charleston at St. Philip's Church on May 23, 1740. The exact date of his birth is unknown. Both his father and grandfather were wealthy Charleston merchants, planters, and public servants. As such, Guerard enjoyed a privileged upbringing and went to England in 1756 to study law at Lincoln's Inn. He was admitted to the South Carolina Bar on January 9, 1761, and set out to follow in the footsteps of his forebears. On November 30, 1766, Guerard married Sarah Middleton. Their marriage was childless.

Guerard represented St. Michael's Parish in the Commons House of Assembly from 1765 to 1768, but spent most of the late 1760s and early 1770s in litigation involving him as the executor of the vast estates of his father and Middleton in-laws. During the Revolutionary War, Guerard lent over £20,000 to the state and served in the militia. After Charleston fell to the British in May 1780, Guerard and other prominent Carolinians were held captive on the prison ship *Pack Horse*. While a prisoner, Guerard attempted to raise funds for the relief of his fellow captives and offered his estate to the British as security. Since the estate had been confiscated, the gesture was rejected by the British but was not soon forgotten by those Guerard had tried to help.

Although he maintained a town house in Charleston, by 1778 Guerard listed St. Helena's Parish as his legal residence and the remainder of his public career was associated with this place. Between 1779 and 1786, Guerard represented the parish four times in the General Assembly: three times in the state House of Representatives and once in the state Senate. In early 1783, Guerard was elected governor by the General Assembly, many members of which were ex-prisoners of war. As governor, Guerard pledged to lead South Carolina "from the Calamities of the uncommonly cruel War" into the "Return of the Blessings of Peace." The task he faced was daunting. South Carolina was deeply in debt and its population, stewing in old war animosities and class antagonism, was badly divided. The governor sought to suppress outlaws plaguing the backcountry and to provide "some small relief" for Charleston's poor. He also led the move to incorporate Charleston in 1783. But while taking a conciliatory stand on most issues, other actions made Guerard some powerful enemies. In an address to the General Assembly on February 2, 1784, he attacked the influential Society of the Cincinnati as aristocratic and undemocratic because membership was based on descent through the eldest line from Continental army officers. A year later, the Pinckney-Middleton-Rutledge political faction saw to the election General William Moultrie, president of the South Carolina Society of the Cincinnati, as Guerard's successor in the governor's chair.

On April 7, 1786, the widower Guerard married Marianne Kennan and retired to Fountainbleu, his 1,474-acre plantation on Goose Creek. Their marriage was also childless. Guerard died on December 21, 1788. MATTHEW A. LOCKHART

Bailey, N. Louise, Mary L. Morgan, and Carolyn R. Taylor, eds. *Biographical Directory of the South Carolina Senate, 1776–1985.* 3 vols. Columbia: University of South Carolina Press, 1986.

Nadelhaft, Jerome J. *The Disorders of War: The Revolution in South Carolina.* Orono: University of Maine Press, 1981.

HAMILTON, PAUL (1762–1816). Governor, secretary of the navy. Hamilton was born in St. Paul's Parish on October 16, 1762, the son of Archibald Hamilton and Rebecca Branford. He received instruction from a private tutor in Charleston until 1778, when he left the city to join a local militia company. During the Revolutionary War, Hamilton served in militia units commanded by Francis Marion and William Harden. He participated in several significant actions, including the siege of Savannah (1779), the Battle of

Camden (1780), and the capture of Fort Balfour (1781). After the war Hamilton took up planting rice and indigo in St. Paul's and St. Bartholomew's Parishes. By 1788 he owned at least thirty-eight slaves and 1,602 acres of land. On October 10, 1782, he married Mary Wilkinson, and the couple eventually had at least six children.

Well positioned by his military service and family connections, Hamilton turned to politics in the postwar years. He served one term in the General Assembly as a representative from St. Paul's Parish from 1787 to 1789. As a delegate to the South Carolina ratification convention in 1788, Hamilton voted in favor of the federal Constitution. He then represented St. Bartholomew's Parish for three terms in the state Senate during the 1790s, during which time he became a Democratic-Republican in contrast to the Federalist leanings of many of his Lowcountry contemporaries. He was an elector for Thomas Jefferson in the 1800 presidential election. While serving as state comptroller of finance, Hamilton was elected governor of South Carolina by the General Assembly on December 10, 1804. During his two-year tenure he advocated military preparedness through improvements to state militia laws and coastal defenses. He also called for a revision of the penal code, requesting that the state's "old sanguinary provincial system" be replaced with a penitentiary system that would provide inmates "time for reflection and amendment." He also urged the General Assembly to ban the Atlantic slave trade, which had been reopened in 1803. Legislators resisted Hamilton's request, however, and the trade remained open until Congress closed it permanently in 1808.

In 1809 President James Madison selected Hamilton to be his secretary of the navy as part of an effort to achieve regional balance in his cabinet appointments. Hamilton proved an inexperienced but competent naval administrator. He advocated fiscal restraint and general military preparedness, including the enlargement of the seventeen-ship U.S. Navy. His one lasting success was in securing congressional support for the creation of a system of naval hospitals in 1811. When war broke out with Britain in 1812, Hamilton, fearing the tiny U.S. Navy would be destroyed, advised Madison to order all vessels to port. He was overruled and Madison implemented a plan to harass British merchant ships. At a presidential ball to celebrate the surrender of HMS *Macedonia,* Hamilton appeared so drunk that Madison requested his resignation. Hamilton subsequently resigned on December 31, 1812. He died at Beaufort on June 30, 1816, and was buried at a private cemetery in Beaufort District. JAMES SPADY

Bailey, N. Louise, Mary L. Morgan, and Carolyn R. Taylor, eds. *Biographical Directory of the South Carolina Senate, 1776–1985.* 3 vols. Columbia: University of South Carolina Press, 1986.

HAMPTON, WADE, I (1754–1835). Planter, soldier, politician. Hampton was born on May 3, 1754, in Virginia, the youngest son of Anthony Hampton and Elizabeth Preston. The family soon after migrated to North Carolina. In the early 1770s several of the Hampton brothers relocated to Ninety Six District, South Carolina, and by April 1774, Wade, along with his parents and other relatives, had moved to the Tyger River valley in present-day Spartanburg County. The brothers were involved in mercantile ventures and trade with the Cherokee Indians in the years before the Revolutionary War. Wade's parents and other family members were killed by an Indian raiding party in late June 1776.

From the beginning of the Revolutionary War, Hampton supported the patriot cause. From 1777 until early 1780 he was an officer and paymaster in the Sixth Continental Regiment. After the fall of Charleston, Hampton signed an oath of allegiance to the British, but used his position as a storekeeper in the Congarees to spy on the British garrison at Granby. Early in 1781 Hampton joined Thomas Sumter as commander of one of the regiments of state troops and took part in the battles at Quinby Bridge (July 17, 1781), Eutaw Springs (September 8, 1781), and Dorchester (December 1, 1781).

Hampton was elected to the General Assembly in 1779, serving several more terms in the 1780s and 1790s. He was also twice elected to the U.S. House of Representatives (1795–1797; 1803–1805) and held other positions of responsibility, including trustee of the South Carolina College (1801–1809). With war again pending with Great Britain in the early 1800s, Hampton again volunteered for military service. He was commissioned as a colonel in the U.S. Army on October 10, 1808. Subsequently promoted to brigadier general (1809) and major general (1813), Hampton served until April 6, 1814, when he resigned after a failed effort to capture Montreal—in conjunction with James Wilkinson—had brought stinging criticism of both men.

Hampton's most lasting fame came from his success as a planter. In 1783 he acquired property on the Congaree River in Richland District, directing much of his time and financial resources to the improvement of his plantations and the more efficient production of his crops. Between 1783 and 1815 he added to his Richland holdings and constantly improved his property, establishing his immensely profitable cotton plantation, Woodlands. In 1799 he produced some six hundred bags of cotton worth an estimated $90,000.

During the first decade of the nineteenth century, his Richland District lands produced on average fifteen hundred bales of cotton each year. In 1811 he purchased land in Louisiana that he developed into one of the most productive sugar plantations on the Mississippi. In 1827 sugar and molasses sales from his Louisiana plantations brought him $100,000 annually, making him that state's largest sugar producer. Noted by *Niles' Weekly Register* in 1823 as "probably the richest planter in the South," Hampton had become a national symbol of the wealthy southern slaveowner. He may have owned as many as nine hundred slaves by 1820 in South Carolina and Louisiana.

Hampton married three times. His first wife, Martha Epps Goodwyn, died in May 1784 after only a year of marriage and left no children. Harriet Flud, who married Hampton in August 1786, left two sons at her death in 1794. He married his third wife, Mary Cantey (Harriet Flud's stepsister), in 1801. The third marriage produced six children. Wade Hampton died February 4, 1835, and was buried in Trinity Churchyard, Columbia. RONALD E. BRIDWELL

Bailey, N. Louise, and Elizabeth Ivey Cooper, eds. *Biographical Directory of the South Carolina House of Representatives.* Vol. 3, *1775–1790.* Columbia: University of South Carolina Press, 1981.

Bridwell, Ronald E. "The South's Wealthiest Planter: Wade Hampton I of South Carolina, 1754–1835." Ph.D. diss., University of South Carolina, 1980.

Cauthen, Charles E., ed. *Family Letters of the Three Wade Hamptons, 1782–1901.* Columbia: University of South Carolina Press, 1953.

Meynard, Virginia G. *The Venturers: The Hampton, Harrison, and Earle Families of Virginia, South Carolina, and Texas.* Easley, S.C.: Southern Historical Press, 1981.

HANGING ROCK, BATTLE OF (August 6, 1780). After the capitulation of Charleston in May 1780, the British moved quickly to gain a foothold in the South Carolina backcountry. Hanging Rock, so named for a large boulder perched on a knob, was one of several outposts situated to protect the main British base at Camden. The stronghold was nothing more than an open field encampment protected by a makeshift earthen berm. Major William Richardson Davie led a successful partisan raid on the outpost on July 30, 1780. Colonel Thomas Sumter planned to follow up with a full assault on Hanging Rock for the morning of August 6. In avoiding an enemy sentry, the patriots' line of march took them too far right for a frontal attack. However, they struck a concentrated blow on the vulnerable British left, where the surprised North Carolinian Volunteers fell back in disorder. Pressing the attack, Sumter's men pushed through to the center of the line. At the height of the battle, the Prince of Wales' American Regiment rallied and regrouped, unperceived under the protection of the woods, and poured a deadly fire on the Americans. The Americans returned the fire so effectively that the Loyalist regiment was almost obliterated. This action allowed the detachment of the British Legion on the British right to form a hollow square defense. Moreover, many partisan soldiers stopped fighting to loot the British camp. Sumter learned of the approach of forty dragoons from Rocky Mount and ordered a withdrawal with minimal losses, leaving behind not quite two hundred British killed and wounded. The Battle of Hanging Rock, though not a complete victory, was a significant setback for British forces in the backcountry. SAMUEL K. FORE

Davie, William R. *The Revolutionary War Sketches of William R. Davie.* Edited by Blackwell P. Robinson. Raleigh: North Carolina Department of Cultural Resources, Division of Archives and History, 1976.
Edgar, Walter. *Partisans and Redcoats: The Southern Conflict That Turned the Tide of the American Revolution.* New York: Morrow, 2001.
Lumpkin, Henry. *From Savannah to Yorktown: The American Revolution in the South.* Columbia: University of South Carolina Press, 1981.

HARDEN, WILLIAM (1743–1785). Soldier. Harden was born on November 8, 1743, in Prince William's Parish, the son of William Harden and Mary Eberson. A landed planter, he entered military service in the militia of colonial Granville County, rising to the rank of captain by the outbreak of the Revolutionary War. He was elected captain of the Beaufort Volunteer Artillery Company on June 17, 1775, which was later incorporated into the Fourth South Carolina Regiment of the Continental Line in January 1776. Harden was appointed to command Fort Lyttelton near Beaufort, a post he held until April 1777. In the spring of 1779 he was promoted to the rank of colonel, commanding the Regiment of Upper Granville County.

Harden was captured in the fall of Charleston in May 1780 and paroled to his plantation near Beaufort. He chose to ignore his parole and after a few months began to actively recruit a partisan force in the Combahee River region. Harden joined the forces assembling under Francis Marion in late 1780 and returned shortly thereafter to harass the enemy in the districts south of Charleston. In April 1781 Harden's force captured and paroled a Loyalist captain and twenty-five men at a muster field at Four Holes. The following evening a detachment of Harden's regiment forced the surrender of a Loyalist post at Red Hill. Continuing their march, Harden's force suffered a setback at the hands of Colonel Thomas Fenwick at Saltketcher Bridge. After a few days' rest, Harden pressed forward toward Fort Balfour, the only major

British fortification between Charleston and the Savannah River. Colonel Fenwick, the fort's commander, was captured outside the fort. After a few hours of negotiation, Harden forced the surrender of the fort without a shot being fired.

Harden's command was not without criticism, however. Governor John Rutledge complained to General Nathanael Greene that Harden, although a "very worthy brave Man," was no disciplinarian, allowing his men to "do as they please." Rutledge later appointed John Barnwell to be brigadier general of the newly created southern militia brigade and Harden, feeling slighted, resigned his commission in November 1781. Although his leadership was not of the same caliber as Marion or Thomas Sumter, Harden nonetheless played an important role in reclaiming South Carolina from British control.

Harden was elected a senator for Prince William's Parish and was present at the Jacksonborough Assembly in January 1782. He married twice, first to Sarah Reid, then to Sarah Cussings. The marriages produced at least four children. Harden held other political offices in Beaufort District before his death on November 28, 1785, in Prince William's Parish. SAMUEL K. FORE

Brown, Tarleton. *Memoirs of Tarleton Brown: A Captain in the Revolutionary Army, Written by Himself.* Edited by Terry W. Lipscomb. Barnwell, S.C.: Barnwell County Museum and Historical Board, 1999.

Daso, Dik A. "Colonel William Harden: The Unsung Partisan Commander." *Proceedings of the South Carolina Historical Association* (1995): 95–111.

Rowland, Lawrence S., Alexander Moore, and George C. Rogers. *The History of Beaufort County, South Carolina.* Vol. 1, *1514–1861.* Columbia: University of South Carolina Press, 1996.

HART, OLIVER (1723–1795). Clergyman. Oliver Hart was born in Warminster, Pennsylvania, on July 5, 1723. He was one of the most influential religious, social, and political leaders of the pre–Revolutionary War South. He began his adult life as a carpenter, though he was also licensed to preach by the Philadelphia Association (Baptist) in 1746. In 1749, after receiving a request from the Charleston Baptist Church for help in locating a pastor, the association encouraged Hart to answer the call and ordained him to the ministry. The Charleston church accepted Hart's unannounced arrival as a sign from God and installed him as minister in 1750, despite his meager education. He would hold that position for thirty years, leading the church in the Regular Baptist tradition. The church's trust was well placed. After educating himself, Hart became a leader not only to his congregation but to Baptists in the entire region. His Regular Baptist heritage inspired him to recruit worthy young men, including Richard Furman, to enter the ministry and to challenge the Charleston Association and the Charleston Religious Society to raise the funds needed for the education of these ministerial prospects.

Even more significant is Hart's influence on denominational organization. In 1749, before Hart left Pennsylvania, he was one of the twenty-nine signers of a document adopted by the Philadelphia Association on the place and authority of an association in Baptist life. The association, as an organizational form, advocates a single denominational structure to support missions and ministry in a geographical area, as opposed to the society form of organization, which creates multiple organizations for the support of a variety of ministries. Hart brought associational organization to South Carolina, and Baptists in the state would in turn advocate it for the Southern Baptist Convention.

Hart also become a champion of liberty, equality, and cooperation among Christians. He encouraged ministers to preach to Native Americans (thereby recognizing their humanity), and he opposed slavery. He wrote in 1754, "Oh that all Bigotry was rooted out of the earth." In 1775 Hart's involvement in the Revolutionary cause, especially in the recruitment of support for the patriots, both in Charleston and in the backcountry, forced him to flee for a time with his family to the Euhaw tribal lands. By 1777, with the support of Baptist leaders in Virginia, Hart became an activist for religious liberty in South Carolina. In 1780 he was driven once again to the Euhaws by the British advance. From there he went to Hopewell, New Jersey, where he served as pastor until his death. Hart never returned to Charleston, though Richard Furman who succeeded him in the pulpit at Charleston expressed a willingness to step down in deference to his leadership at any time.

Hart was married twice, first to Sarah Brees in 1747, who was the mother of four children who survived infancy (Eleanor, Oliver, John, Mary Baker). His second marriage in 1774 was to Anne Sealey Grimball, who gave him one son, William Rogers. Hart died in Hopewell, New Jersey, on December 31, 1795, and was buried in the Southampton Old School Baptist Cemetery in Southampton, Pennsylvania. HELEN LEE TURNER

Hart, Oliver. Papers. Baptist Historical Collection, Furman University, Greenville.
Owens, Loulie Latimer. *Oliver Hart, 1723–1795: A Biography.* Greenville, S.C.: South Carolina Baptist Historical Society, 1966.

HEYWARD, THOMAS, JR. (1746–1809). Planter, legislator, jurist, signer of the Declaration of Independence. Heyward (designated "Jr." to distinguish him from others of that name in his family), the eldest son of Daniel Heyward

Thomas Heyward, Jr.
Courtesy, National Portrait
Gallery, Smithsonian
Institution.

and Maria Miles, was born on July 28, 1746, at his father's Old House plantation in St. Helena's Parish. After receiving a classical education, he was sent to London to study law at the Middle Temple in 1765. Returning to South Carolina in 1771, Heyward was admitted to the Charleston Bar on January 22, 1771, and was practicing law in Charleston when elected to represent St. Helena's Parish in the Commons House of Assembly.

Heyward took an active role in opposition to British rule and served on the Committee of Ninety-Nine in 1774, which called for the formation of the First Provincial Congress the following year. He was additionally one of the thirteen members appointed to the Council of Safety and was reelected to the Second Provincial Congress in late 1775, which resolved itself into the First General Assembly in 1776. The Second Provincial Congress reappointed Heyward to the Council of Safety. Early in 1776 he was chosen to replace the resigning Christopher Gadsden in the Second Continental Congress. That summer Thomas Heyward, Jr., was one of four South Carolinians who signed the Declaration of Independence in Philadelphia.

Sitting in Congress for two years, Heyward returned to South Carolina in 1778 and was appointed a circuit judge in 1779, a position he held for ten years. In that capacity he upheld the confiscation and amercement of Loyalist property after the Revolutionary War. Heyward's political responsibilities did not prevent his military duty. As a captain in the Charleston Artillery Company, he was wounded in the successful defense at Port Royal Island in

February 1779. Captured at the head of his battery at the fall of Charleston, Heyward was paroled, but was later recalled and imprisoned at St. Augustine, Florida. Exchanged and sent to Philadelphia, he returned to South Carolina and was elected to the Fourth General Assembly in 1782. Heyward was also a supporter of the federal Constitution and a member of the state convention which ratified it in 1788, and he was a member of the subsequent state constitutional convention.

In 1790 Heyward retired from active public life in order to devote himself to his family and agricultural pursuits at his White Hall Plantation in St. Luke's Parish. He had been a founder and the first president of the Agricultural Society of South Carolina and continued to work with the society until his death. He married twice. On April 20, 1773, he married Elizabeth Mathewes, who died in 1782. On May 4, 1786, Heyward married Elizabeth Savage. Together the marriages produced eight children. Thomas Heyward, Jr., died on April 22, 1809, and was buried in the family cemetery on Old House Plantation in St. Luke's Parish. SAMUEL K. FORE

Edgar, Walter, and N. Louise Bailey, eds. *Biographical Directory of the South Carolina House of Representatives.* Vol. 2, *The Commons House of Assembly, 1692–1775.* Columbia: University of South Carolina Press, 1977.

Hemphill, William E., ed. *Extracts from the Journals of the Provincial Congresses of South Carolina, 1775–1776.* Columbia: South Carolina Archives Department, 1960.

Salley, Alexander S. *Delegates to the Continental Congress from South Carolina, 1774–1789, with Sketches of the Four Who Signed the Declaration of Independence.* Columbia, S.C.: State Company, 1927.

HOBKIRK HILL, BATTLE OF (April 25, 1781). Following the Battle of Guilford Courthouse in North Carolina, Major General Nathanael Greene chose not to follow Lord Cornwallis and reentered South Carolina in April of 1781. His plan was to force a British withdrawal from their interior outposts to Charleston. On April 19 his army of some 1,200 Continentals and 250 militia took up a position on Hobkirk Hill, a mile and a half north of Camden.

Francis Lord Rawdon, who commanded the British outpost at Camden, chose to attack the encroaching Americans on April 25. He approached Greene's camp through thick woods and on a narrow front in hope of achieving a surprise. Rawdon's leading forces struck the American picket line at about eleven o'clock in the morning, and the American pickets fought well enough to give Greene time to muster and deploy his forces. Assessing the situation, Greene noted the narrow front of the British column and proposed to launch a double envelopment. But Rawdon quickly brought up his second line and extended his flanks to counter the maneuver. More critically for Greene, the veteran First Maryland Regiment fell into disorder and its commander, Colonel John Gunby, ordered an abrupt withdrawal to reform his unit. The move affected the other units and the American advance faltered, forcing Greene to order a general retreat.

The Americans fell back three miles to the old Camden battlefield and the British were left in possession of the hill. They did not stay there. Rawdon withdrew into his fortification at Camden. Indeed, despite five hundred British reinforcements that arrived two weeks later, Rawdon abandoned his exposed position and began a slow retreat toward Charleston on May 10. Though in itself indecisive, the Battle of Hobkirk Hill marked the beginning of the British withdrawal from the interior of South Carolina. SAMUEL K. FORE

Conrad, Dennis M., and Richard K. Shannon, eds. *The Papers of General Nathanael Greene.* Vol. 8, *30 March–10 July 1781.* Chapel Hill: University of North Carolina Press, 1995.

Kirkland, Thomas J., and Robert M. Kennedy. *Historic Camden.* 2 vols. 1905. Reprint, Camden, S.C.: Kershaw County Historical Society, 1994.

Lumpkin, Henry. *From Savannah to Yorktown: The American Revolution in the South.* Columbia: University of South Carolina Press, 1981.

HORRY, PETER (ca. 1743–1815). Planter, soldier, legislator. Horry was born on March 12, 1743 or 1744, in Prince George Winyah Parish, the son of the Huguenot rice planter John Horry. Educated at the Indigo Society's free school in Georgetown, Peter Horry later served a harsh apprenticeship with a local merchant. By the late 1760s Horry had established a mercantile partnership in Georgetown, which he gave up on inheriting 475 acres from his father. Eventually Horry owned plantations on Winyah Bay and the Santee River as well as land in Ninety Six District and a house in Columbia (later called the Horry-Guignard House). At his death he owned as many as 116 slaves.

Horry's military service began during the Revolutionary War when he was commissioned a captain on June 12, 1775. He served with Francis Marion in the Second South Carolina, which distinguished itself at the Battle of Sullivan's Island in June 1776. After the battle Horry was promoted to major and, in 1779, to lieutenant colonel in the Continental army. In January 1780 he took command of the Fifth South Carolina, with the rank of colonel in the state militia. When the Fifth and other undermanned regiments were merged, Horry's services were not needed and he was released from active duty. At home when Charleston fell in May 1780, Horry went to North Carolina and joined General Johann de Kalb's staff as an observer. In the summer of 1780 he returned to South Carolina and served as one of Marion's most valuable and trusted officers. Late in the war, when Marion attended the legislature at Jacksonborough, he left Horry in command of his brigade. In the meantime, General Nathanael Greene had created two battalions of light cavalry, one commanded by Horry and the other by Hezekiah Maham. Since their new commissions as lieutenant colonels bore the same date, a feud developed between the two men, one result of which was the defeat of Marion's brigade in late February 1782 at Wambaw Bridge. After the two regiments were consolidated under Maham, Horry was appointed commandant at Georgetown, a port vital to Greene's army.

After the war Horry remained in the military service of the state. In 1792 he was given command of the Sixth militia brigade. In 1798 the brigade mobilized to face a rumored invasion by French forces and again in 1802 against a potential slave revolt. He retired from the militia in 1806. A member of the Society of the Cincinnati, Horry collected a sizable archive of war documents and letters. He gave them to Mason Locke "Parson" Weems, fresh from his popular, but contrived, biography of George Washington. Weems took so many liberties in writing the *Life of Marion* (1809) that Horry disassociated himself from the work. Horry also kept a journal from 1812 until shortly before his death, parts of which were published in the 1930s and 1940s in the *South Carolina Historical and Genealogical Magazine.*

Horry represented Prince George Winyah Parish in the state House of Representatives in 1782 and from 1792 to 1794. He sat in the state Senate for the same parish from 1785 to 1787. In 1801, when the legislature established new judicial districts, the state honored his war-time service by creating Horry District.

Horry married Margaret Magdalen Guignard on February 9, 1793, a union that produced no children. He died in Columbia on February 28, 1815, and was buried at Trinity Church, Columbia. ROY TALBERT, JR.

Bailey, N. Louise, Mary L. Morgan, and Carolyn R. Taylor, eds. *Biographical Directory of the South Carolina Senate, 1776–1985.* 3 vols. Columbia: University of South Carolina Press, 1986.

Salley, Alexander S., ed. "The Journal of General Peter Horry." *South Carolina Historical and Genealogical Magazine* 38–48 (April 1937–April 1947).

———. "Horry's Notes to Weems's *Life of Marion.*" *South Carolina Historical and Genealogical Magazine* 61 (July 1960): 119–22.

HUCK, CHRISTIAN (?–1780). Soldier. Christian Huck, a Loyalist captain of dragoons under Banastre Tarleton, gained notoriety in South Carolina during the Revolutionary War for his vicious acts and excessive use of profanity. A Philadelphia lawyer, Huck was known for his intense hatred of all patriots, especially Scots-Irish Presbyterians, whom he considered the most sympathetic to the rebels. After joining the ranks of the British in New York, he commanded British outposts around Camden, South Carolina, and participated in other actions involving Tarleton's Legion.

In June 1780 Huck and a portion of his command were sent from Rocky Mount toward the vicinity of Fishing Creek to disperse the rebels in that area. Along the way Huck recruited three hundred Loyalists and burned the houses and plantations of known patriots who lived in the Catawba Valley of upper South Carolina. At Fishing Creek, Huck turned his force toward the local church in hopes of capturing Presbyterian pastor and patriot John Simpson. Not finding Simpson, the Tories burned his home to the ground. Huck's command continued its rampage in the New Acquisition District (York County) by destroying White's Mills on Fishing Creek and William Hill's Iron Works, a strategic source of cannon and ordnance for the patriots.

While Huck was wreaking havoc throughout the countryside, five hundred loosely organized patriots set out to find and destroy Huck. One patriot, John McClure, had his home destroyed by Huck, and his family was treated savagely and held as prisoners. One of his daughters managed to elude the captors and brought word to the American camp about the outrages that had occurred. With advance warning of the approach of the Tories and the knowledge of their whereabouts, the patriots went searching for Huck.

Before dawn on July 12, 1780, a force of 250 patriots commanded by Colonel William Bratton tracked Huck down at Williamson's Plantation, located a little more than fifty miles northeast of Camden in the New Acquisition District. Huck had camped his men on poor ground and failed to put out patrols or pickets. Although he had posted sentries on the road in front of the plantation house, they did not hear the approach of the rebels. As a result the Tories, many of whom were still asleep, were taken completely by surprise and easily defeated. When he tried to escape on horse bareback, Huck was shot in the neck and fell from his horse. The wound proved mortal, and Huck died later that day. The majority of his command were either captured or killed.

"Huck's Defeat"—as the battle at Williamson's Plantation came to be known—proved to the patriots that they could measure up to British regulars and that Tarleton's feared legion was not as imposing as they had once thought. After Huck's defeat the patriot ranks swelled with new recruits. KENDRA DEBANY

Buchanan, John. *The Road to Guilford Courthouse: The American Revolution in the Carolinas.* New York: Wiley, 1997.

Edgar, Walter. *Partisans and Redcoats: The Southern Conflict That Turned the Tide of the American Revolution.* New York: Morrow, 2001.

Morrill, Dan L. *Southern Campaigns of the American Revolution.* Baltimore: Nautical & Aviation Publishing, 1993.

Russell, David Lee. *The American Revolution in the Southern Colonies.* Jefferson, N.C.: McFarland, 2000.

HUGER, ISAAC (1743–1797). Soldier. Huger was born on March 19, 1743, at Limerick Plantation on the Cooper River, the second son of Daniel Huger, a Huguenot merchant and planter, and Mary Cordes. The wealth of his family afforded Huger, along with his brothers, an education in Europe. Huger began his military career by serving as an officer in Colonel Thomas Middleton's Provincial South Carolina Regiment during the expedition against the Cherokees in the spring of 1761. On March 23, 1762, Huger married Elizabeth Chalmers. The couple had eight children.

While serving as a representative for the parishes of St. Philip's and St. Michael's in the First Provincial Congress, Huger was appointed a lieutenant colonel in the South Carolina militia and later commissioned a lieutenant colonel in the First South Carolina Regiment on June 17, 1775. He was promoted to colonel on September 16, 1776, and appointed commander of the Fifth South Carolina Regiment. On January 9, 1779, he was promoted to the rank of brigadier general in the Continental army.

Huger fought and was wounded at the Battle of Stono Ferry on June 20, 1779, and commanded the South Carolina and Georgia militia during the siege of Savannah on October 9, 1779. During the siege of Charleston in the spring of 1780, he was placed in command of the light horse and militia outside the city. A surprise attack by Lieutenant Colonel Banastre Tarleton's forces routed and dispersed Huger's troops at Moncks Corner on the morning of April 14, 1780. Illness kept Huger from capture with the surrender of Charleston, and he later rejoined the southern army under Major General Horatio Gates in North Carolina.

Huger was present when Major General Nathanael Greene took command of the Southern Department in Charlotte later in December. Greene detached his light forces to the western parts of South Carolina and moved his regulars to a camp in the Cheraws, with Huger as his second in command. After the brilliant American victory at Cowpens, Huger was entrusted by Greene to lead the command posted in the Cheraws to rejoin the detached light forces in North Carolina. At the Battle of Guilford Courthouse on March 15, 1781, he commanded a brigade of Virginia Continental regiments and was slightly wounded in action. Commanding the same brigade at the Battle of Hobkirk Hill on April 25, Huger initially stood his ground after the unanticipated withdrawal of the right wing of the American line. With the retreat of the British from the interior to Charleston, Huger was reunited with his family and returned to his home, ending his military service.

Huger represented St. George's Dorchester Parish in the Jacksonborough Assembly in January 1782 and served in the legislature until his election as sheriff of Charleston District in 1785. Familial ties led to his appointment as the first federal marshal for South Carolina in 1789, a position which he held for five years. He died in Charleston on October 6, 1797. SAMUEL K. FORE

Edgar, Walter, and N. Louise Bailey, eds. *Biographical Directory of the South Carolina House of Representatives.* Vol. 2, *The Commons House of Assembly, 1692–1775.* Columbia: University of South Carolina Press, 1977.

Johnson, William. *Sketches of the Life and Correspondence of Nathanael Greene.* 2 vols. 1822. Reprint, New York: Da Capo, 1973.

Moultrie, William. *Memoirs of the American Revolution.* 1802. Reprint, New York: New York Times, 1968.

IZARD, RALPH (1742–1804). Diplomat, congressman, legislator, U.S. senator. Izard was born on January 23, 1742, the son of planter Henry Izard and Margaret Johnson, daughter of South Carolina governor Robert Johnson. At the age of twelve, Izard traveled to England, where he first attended Hackney School and later matriculated at Christ College, Cambridge University, in 1761. Returning to South Carolina in December 1764, Izard inherited extensive property in three Lowcountry parishes. He established his home plantation at the Elms, St. James Goose Creek Parish, and built up a beautifully landscaped estate that eventually comprised 2,353 acres. While traveling in New York, Izard met Alice DeLancey, whom he wed on May 1, 1767. The marriage produced fourteen children, seven of whom reached maturity.

In his early years, Izard preferred the life of a cultivated gentleman and did not pursue politics. The Izards moved to London in 1771 and planned to reside in England permanently and live off the income of their South Carolina estates. But the political break between Britain and the American colonies forced the family to move to Paris in 1776.

Izard's presence in Europe made him available for diplomatic service. In May 1777 the Continental Congress elected him commissioner to Tuscany. Because the grand duke of Florence refused to allow representatives of the rebellious colonies into Italy, Izard never made it to Tuscany. He spent the next two years in Paris corresponding with Tuscan officials and becoming entangled in the disputes that divided the official American commissioners in France. Izard developed a particular antipathy toward Benjamin Franklin, which would endure throughout his public career. Frustrated over his status as a diplomat in waiting, Izard resigned in March 1779. Shortly thereafter, Congress recalled him in June 1779 because of his fractured relationship with Franklin and allegations of financial misconduct. On his arrival in Philadelphia in August 1780, Izard explained to Congress the difficulties under which he had operated.

Congress responded by exonerating him. Before returning to South Carolina, Izard visited General George Washington's headquarters and successfully lobbied for the appointment of Nathanael Greene as commander of the Continental army in the Southern Department.

In January 1782 the South Carolina legislature elected Izard to the Continental Congress, where he served until September 1783. Izard supported Congress's attempt to raise revenue through a duty on imports. The Revolutionary War's impact on his personal life affected his public positions. He corresponded with New York political leaders to secure lenient treatment of his mother-in-law, who was a suspected Loyalist. He also strongly insisted that the British abide by the article in the peace treaty that prohibited them from removing American property, particularly slaves. Izard estimated that the British confiscated 170 of his own slaves.

With the war's end, Izard set out to rebuild his damaged property in South Carolina. He succeeded in recouping his losses and by 1790 owned 602 slaves, becoming one of the wealthiest planters of his day. He also speculated in nonagricultural endeavors. Earlier than most of his contemporaries, Izard envisioned canals as a means of developing the South Carolina backcountry and cementing that region's political ties to the Lowcountry. He helped establish the Santee Canal Company in 1786, on one end of which he planned to build "Izardtown" on lands he owned on the Santee River.

Around this time Izard also acquired two politically prominent sons-in-laws, Gabriel Manigault and William Loughton Smith. Together they formed the Izard-Manigault-Smith, or Goose Creek, faction and played a major role in South Carolina politics for more than a decade. Elected to the state House of Representatives five times between 1782 and 1789, Izard emerged as a "planter-boss of the Lowcountry." In December 1786 he exerted his political influence to prevent the election of Thomas Tudor Tucker to the state legislature, resulting in a duel in which Izard shot his opponent in the left thigh. In 1788 Izard helped ensure his son-in-law William Smith's election to the

U.S. House of Representatives by authoring *Another Elector for Charleston District,* a broadside that labeled Smith's opponent, David Ramsay, as antislavery and inimical to South Carolina's economic interests.

Izard soon joined his son-in-law in Congress. In January 1789 the South Carolina legislature elected Izard to the U.S. Senate. In the First Congress, he united with other Carolina congressmen in lobbying for federal assumption of state debts, a policy that relieved South Carolina of a crippling financial burden imposed by the war. He opposed passage of the Bill of Rights and strongly objected to the reception of Quaker antislavery petitions. Concerned over rising antislavery sentiment in the North and Europe, he predicted, "The time is at no very great distance when the property in negroes will be rendered of no value." Izard generally supported the Washington administration, though he firmly opposed any executive encroachment on the Senate's prerogatives. His aristocratic and haughty bearing earned him criticism from many contemporaries. Izard served as president pro tempore of the Third Congress from May 1794 to February 1795. At the conclusion of his term, he retired to South Carolina to manage his plantations. In 1797, Izard suffered a stroke that left him an invalid. He died in Charleston on May 30, 1804, and was buried in the St. James Goose Creek Churchyard. GREGORY D. MASSEY

Bowling, Kenneth R., and Helen E. Veit, eds. *The Diary of William Maclay and Other Notes on Senate Debates.* Baltimore: Johns Hopkins University Press, 1988.

Rogers, George C. *Evolution of a Federalist: William Loughton Smith of Charleston (1758–1812).* Columbia: University of South Carolina Press, 1962.

Smith, Paul H., ed. *Letters of Delegates to Congress, 1774–1789.* Vols. 18–20. Washington, D.C.: Library of Congress, 1991–1993.

JACKSON, ANDREW (1767–1845). Soldier, U.S. senator, president of the United States. Jackson was born in the Waxhaw settlement of Lancaster District on March 15, 1767, the son of Andrew Jackson and Elizabeth Hutchinson. He is the only South Carolinian to serve as president of the United States. Fatherless at birth, Jackson was raised by his mother in the home of relatives and attended local schools. He lost his mother and older brothers during the Revolution to illnesses. His activities against Tories led to his capture by the British in April 1781. During his capture, an officer demanded that young Jackson clean his boots. Jackson's refusal was rewarded with a sword slash that left scars on his head and hand.

In 1784 Jackson moved to Salisbury, North Carolina, to study law, passing the bar in 1787. He then moved west into what would become Tennessee.

Andrew Jackson. Etching on paper, 1908. Courtesy, National Portrait Gallery, Smithsonian Institution.

Settling in Nashville, he quickly gained notice as a prosecutor and attorney. He fell in love with the married, but separated, Rachel Donelson Robards. The murky circumstances over her divorce, with charges of adultery, and the subsequent marriage to Jackson on January 18, 1794, would haunt Jackson during his presidential campaigns.

His wife's prominent family and his own political associations fueled Jackson's rise in politics. He served at Tennessee's constitutional convention in 1796 and as the state's first U.S. Representative. He served one year in the U.S. Senate before winning election to the Tennessee Superior Court. In 1802 he won a bitter election for the prominent position of major general in the militia.

During the War of 1812, Jackson defeated the Creek Indians at Horseshoe Bend in 1814, which led to a commission as major general in the U.S. Army. Ordered to New Orleans, he gathered a mixed force of irregulars to block a British attempt to seize the city. His stunning victory over British regulars made him a national icon. His popularity increased when he invaded Spanish Florida in 1818 and hanged two British subjects accused of agitating Indians along the Alabama-Georgia border. President James Monroe, Secretary of War John C. Calhoun, and the cabinet came close to disavowing Jackson's actions before a treaty purchasing Florida from Spain ended the crisis.

His tremendous popularity made Jackson a presidential contender. Following a short term as territorial governor of Florida, he returned to Tennessee. Nominated for president in 1822 with little initial support, Jackson reluctantly accepted his election by the Tennessee legislature to the U.S. Senate in 1823. Once in Washington, Jackson spoke out against the rampant corruption and intrigue he found there. In the 1824 presidential election, he received the most popular votes, but failed to gather an Electoral College majority. The U.S. House of Representatives, with the support of Speaker Henry Clay, awarded the presidency to John Quincy Adams, who subsequently appointed Clay as Secretary of State. Jackson fumed at this "corrupt bargain" and considered it a deliberate repudiation of the will of the people.

Jackson resigned his Senate seat and returned to Tennessee in 1825. A coalition of antiadministration foes began to form around him and his call for reform. An early and uneasy alliance was made with Calhoun, and Jackson agreed to finance a newspaper run by a Calhoun supporter, Duff Green. Soon, New York's Martin Van Buren and other prominent politicians added their organizational support to Jackson's candidacy, forming the basis of the modern Democratic Party. A vicious campaign ensued in 1828 fueled by rumors regarding his marriage, but Jackson with Calhoun as his vice presidential candidate swept to an overwhelming victory. Jackson advocated limited government, payment of the national debt, removal of the Indians beyond the Mississippi, and rotation of public officials he opposed the monopolistic power of the Second Bank of the United States.

The Jackson administration had a troubled start when Peggy O'Neal Eaton, the wife of his secretary of war, was ostracized by Washington society under the lead of Calhoun's wife, Floride. Concurrently, Calhoun's "Exposition and Protest" against the Tariffs of 1824 and 1828 was published, advocating the right of nullification. Although a supporter of states' rights, Jackson was an ardent nationalist and viewed nullification as the first step towards disunion and a repudiation of majority rule. In reply to Calhoun and the growing nullification sentiment, Jackson, at the 1830 annual Jefferson Dinner declared, "Our Union: It must be preserved."

Jackson soon discovered that Calhoun, as secretary of war, had advocated Jackson's arrest and punishment over his invasion of Florida, furthering the split between the two men. Many saw the intrigue of Van Buren behind the schism as a bid to supplant Calhoun as Jackson's successor. The final break occurred when Jackson arranged for a new newspaper to advocate the administration's policies. An attempted reconciliation imploded when Calhoun published his correspondence over the Florida affair. Jackson subsequently purged his cabinet, an action never previously taken. Van Buren assumed Calhoun's spot on the 1832 ticket, cementing his role as Jackson's successor.

The Tariff of 1832 renewed nullification sentiment in South Carolina, despite a drop in duties. In November a South Carolina convention nullified the tariff acts and prohibited the collection of custom duties within the state. On December 10, 1832, Jackson issued a proclamation declaring the actions "incompatible with the existence of the Union . . . and destructive of the great object for which it was formed" and asked for authorization to use force. The president's nationalistic position galvanized support throughout the nation. A compromise tariff and the Wilkins Act, or Force Bill, were signed into law days before Jackson's second inauguration, ending the crisis as well as the political effectiveness of the nullification threat.

Jackson's popularity among the masses, his strong personality and leadership, and his underappreciated political skills redefined and strengthened the presidency during his two terms. His stand against nullification forced southerners to seek other, more drastic means of redress when slavery became the main sectional issue. Jackson's political opponents coalesced into the Whig Party and firmly established the two-party political system. His command of the Democratic Party led to Van Buren's election as president in 1836. Leaving office in 1837, Jackson retired to his home, the Hermitage, outside of Nashville. He died on June 8, 1845, and was buried in his garden. PATRICK MCCAWLEY

Burstein, Andrew. *The Passions of Andrew Jackson.* New York: Knopf, 2003.
Remini, Robert V. *Andrew Jackson.* 3 vols. New York: Harper & Row, 1977–1984.
Wyatt-Brown, Bertram. *The Shaping of Southern Culture: Honor, Grace, and War, 1760s–1880s.* Chapel Hill: University of North Carolina Press, 2001.

JAMES, JOHN (1732–1791). Soldier, legislator. John James, son of William James and Elizabeth Witherspoon, was born in Ireland on April 12, 1732. The family migrated to Prince Frederick's Parish, South Carolina, shortly after his birth and James grew to be a prominent planter with large landholdings. Before the Revolutionary War, James owned at least 2,114 acres, including 354 acres on the Black River, 950 acres on the Waccamaw River, 710 acres along the Little Pee Dee River and Lynches Creek, and 100 acres near Indiantown in Williamsburg County. He married Jean Dobein on January 18, 1753. They had five children.

James gained his first military experience as a captain in the provincial militia during the Cherokee War (1759–1761). In 1775 and 1776 he participated in the Second Provincial Congress and the First General Assembly, representing Prince Frederick's Parish. At the outbreak of the Revolutionary War, he was elected a captain in the state militia and served in the defense of Charleston under General William Moultrie, commanding a force of 120 men at a skirmish at Tulifinny Bridge in 1779. Fortunately for James, he was not among those who surrendered when the British captured Charleston in May 1780, having been ordered by Governor John Rutledge to raise a militia unit in the Williamsburg Township region.

William Dobein James, John James's second son, relates the story that after the fall of Charleston, the British demanded loyalty oaths from paroled Americans. James was chosen by the local inhabitants to meet with British authorities in Georgetown to ask if the oaths included the obligation to take up arms against their neighbors still in rebellion. Meeting with a British officer in Georgetown, James was told that not only their loyalty but also their service for the king was demanded. The unarmed James, believing he was being threatened, retreated from the meeting brandishing a chair in front of him. Once clear of the officer, he returned to Williamsburg to report the event. The news of this incident, and that of General Horatio Gates arriving in North Carolina to take charge of a new American army, induced the Williamsburg patriots to return to arms against the British. Once again, James was elected to lead them.

James turned his militia force over to Francis Marion in August 1781 at Witherspoon's Ferry on Lynches Creek. James served under Marion as a major and took part in several skirmishes against the British, including the Battle of Eutaw Springs (September 8, 1781). Shortly after the battle, he was elected to the state legislature and served in the Fourth General Assembly (1782). After the Revolution, he worked to restore his properties, which were heavily damaged during the war, and was again elected to public service, representing Prince Frederick's Parish in the Sixth General Assembly (1785–1786). James died on January 29, 1791, and was buried at Indiantown Presbyterian Church. STEVEN D. SMITH

Bailey, N. Louise, and Elizabeth Ivey Cooper, eds. *Biographical Directory of the South Carolina House of Representatives.* Vol. 3, *1775–1790.* Columbia: University of South Carolina Press, 1981.

Blanchard, Amos. *American Military Biography: Containing the Lives and Characters of the Officers of the Revolution, Who Were Most Distinguished in Achieving our National Independence.* New York: Edward J. Swords, 1830.

James, William Dobein. *A Sketch of the Life of Brig. Gen. Francis Marion*. 1821. Reprint, Marietta, Ga.: Continental Book Company, 1948.

JASPER, WILLIAM (?–1779). Soldier. Little is known of Jasper's origins. Traditionally he has been identified as Irish, but others have argued that he was of German ancestry.

On July 7, 1775, in Halifax District, Georgia, William Jasper enlisted in the elite grenadier company of the Second South Carolina Continental Regiment. On June 28, 1776, as a sergeant, he won lasting fame during the British attack on Sullivan's Island, near Charleston. When an enemy shot brought down the fort's flag, Jasper restored the banner while under enemy fire. In 1779 he led dangerous guerrilla raids against British pickets and patrols. At least once, he passed through enemy lines by posing as a deserter. During the Franco-American attack on the British lines around Savannah on October 9, 1779, Jasper received a mortal wound while rescuing one of his regiment's flags. He had placed another flag on a British entrenchment, which is now preserved in the Smithsonian Institution. Jasper left a widow and at least two children, although apparently no descendants are living today.

William Jasper. Courtesy, New York Public Library.

Jasper became a national hero as a character in the historical novel by Mason L. Weems, *The Life of Gen. Francis Marion* (1809). Weems based this work loosely on a manuscript by Peter Horry. Although Horry dismissed Weems's book, he and other Revolutionary War veterans confirmed Jasper's great personal courage. Eight counties (including Jasper County, South Carolina), numerous towns, and thousands of Americans were named for the man described as "the Brave Sergt. Jasper." ROBERT S. DAVIS

Gamble, Thomas. "The Story of Sergeant William Jasper, Hero of the Revolution: 1775 to 1779." Scrapbook. Georgia Department of Archives and History, Morrow, Georgia.
Jones, George Fenwick. "Sergeant Johann Wilhelm Jasper." *Georgia Historical Quarterly* 65 (spring 1981): 7–15.

JEREMIAH, THOMAS (?–1775). Free black harbor pilot, alleged insurrectionary. Thomas Jeremiah, or "Jerry," was a free person of color who earned a living by navigating ships through the treacherous waters of Charleston harbor. Little is known about his life. It appears that he obtained his freedom sometime in the mid-to-late eighteenth century. In addition to his skills as a harbor pilot, Jeremiah worked as a firefighter and ran the fish market in Charleston's wharf district. Eventually he would become a slaveowner himself, acquiring an estate valued at somewhere between £700 to £1,000 sterling. Earning the respect of his own community as well as a number of prominent white allies, the pilot undoubtedly blurred and transcended the boundaries of race that were becoming ever more sharply drawn during the course of his lifetime. Yet the same skills which initially brought him success and notoriety would ultimately make him a target for suspicion.

Jeremiah's paradoxical relationship to the power structure is perhaps best illustrated by an incident that occurred in 1771. On July 17, he was convicted of assaulting a white ship captain by the name of Thomas Langen—a bold action for a black man living in the pre-Revolutionary South—and was sentenced to an hour in the pillory and ten lashes with a whip. In view of his public deeds, however, Lieutenant Governor William Bull granted him a pardon. Four years later, when open conflict broke out between Great Britain and her North American colonies, Jeremiah would not be so lucky.

In June 1775, he became the foremost suspect in an alleged plot by the British to use the majority of the Carolina populace—enslaved blacks—against the patriot rebels. As a man who had long worked with battleships and fire, Jeremiah appeared to be the most plausible and potentially dangerous link between black Carolinians and the British. Embroiled in a cause célèbre between the last royal governor of South Carolina, Lord William Campbell, and patriot leader Henry Laurens, Thomas Jeremiah was adjudged guilty by patriot authorities and sentenced to die under the Negro Act of 1740.

On August 18, 1775, at twelve o'clock noon, Jeremiah was brought before the gallows in Charleston. Before the noose could be tightened around his neck, he proclaimed his innocence and told his accusers that "God's judgment would one day overtake them for shedding his innocent blood." While the rest of spectacle is difficult to piece together, Jeremiah reportedly met "death like a man and a Christian." After he was asphyxiated, his remains were set on fire—both a reminder and a warning. "Surely," one contemporary concluded, "there is no murder so cruel and dangerous as that committed under the appearance of law and justice." Although we may never know whether he was "guilty" or "innocent," Jeremiah's ordeal illustrated the three-way struggle for power among blacks, Whigs, and Tories that was taking place throughout the lower South on the eve of the Revolutionary War. WILLIAM RYAN

Ryan, William R. "'Under the Color of Law': The Ordeal of Thomas Jeremiah, a Free Black Man, and the Struggle for Power in Revolutionary South Carolina." In *George Washington's South,* edited by Tamara Harvey and Greg O'Brien. Gainesville: University Press of Florida, 2004.

Wood, Peter H. "'Liberty is Sweet': African-American Freedom Struggles in the Years before White Independence." In *Beyond the American Revolution: Explorations in the History of American Radicalism,* edited by Alfred F. Young. DeKalb: Northern Illinois University Press, 1993.

———. "'Taking Care of Business' in Revolutionary South Carolina: Republicanism and the Slave Society." In *The Southern Experience in the American Revolution,* edited by Jeffrey J. Crow and Larry E. Tise. Chapel Hill: University of North Carolina Press, 1978.

KERSHAW, JOSEPH (ca. 1727–1791). Merchant. Kershaw was born in Yorkshire, England, the eldest son of Joseph Kershaw. Little is known about his early years. Around the mid-1750s he and two brothers, Ely and William, immigrated to South Carolina. Joseph became a clerk for the Charleston merchant James Laurens, the elder brother of Henry Laurens. In 1758, however, Kershaw struck out for the colony's interior, establishing a store northwest of Charleston near the Wateree River at Pine Tree Hill. There, acting as an agent for the Charleston firm of Ancrum, Lance, & Loocock, Kershaw laid the foundations for his future success. On October 20, 1762, he married Sarah Mathis. The couple had eight children.

In 1763 Kershaw formed a partnership with his brother Ely, John Chesnut, William Ancrum, and Aaron Loocock. Centered in Charleston, the partnership used Kershaw to provide a base of operations to expand its trade into the interior. Although the partnership experienced mixed success, Kershaw's own mercantile operations made him the leading commercial, and subsequently political, figure in the Wateree River region. His business operations expanded to include a large flour and grist mill, indigo works, a warehouse, a brewery, and a distillery. He and his partners also acquired grants for several thousands of acres of land across the colony. In 1769 Kershaw played a lead role in convincing his Pine Tree Hill neighbors to lay out a series of streets and lots, which became the town of Camden.

Kershaw was elected to the Commons House of Assembly in 1769, in which he was a member of the committee that drew up the Circuit Court Act, which established several new judicial districts in the interior. He was returned to three more assemblies before the start of the Revolutionary War and then was elected to the First (1775) and Second (1775–1776) Provincial Congresses and the first five General Assemblies (1776–1784). As a legislator and militia officer, Kershaw worked to secure interior settlers and Catawba Indians to the patriot cause. A major and later a colonel in the state militia, Kershaw saw action at Purrysburg and Stono River and was captured at the Battle of Camden (August 1780). He was imprisoned at British Honduras and then Bermuda, where he nevertheless was able to mortgage his Carolina lands to secure needed supplies for American forces (the vessel carrying the cargo was unfortunately captured). He was eventually exchanged and returned to South Carolina.

Kershaw spent the last years of his life trying to rebuild his war-torn business enterprises in Camden. He died on December 28, 1791, and was buried in the town's Episcopal cemetery. That year Kershaw County was named in his honor. TOM DOWNEY

Bailey, N. Louise, Mary L. Morgan, and Carolyn R. Taylor, eds. *Biographical Directory of the South Carolina Senate, 1776–1985.* 3 vols. Columbia: University of South Carolina Press, 1986.

Ernst, Joseph A., and H. Roy Merrens. "'Camden's Turrets Pierce the Skies!': The Urban Process in the Southern Colonies during the Eighteenth Century." *William and Mary Quarterly,* 3d ser., 30 (October 1973): 549–74.

Kirkland, Thomas J., and Robert M. Kennedy. *Historic Camden.* 2 vols. 1905. Reprint, Camden, S.C.: Kershaw County Historical Society, 1994.

KINGS MOUNTAIN, BATTLE OF (October 7, 1780). On September 12, 1780, the British major Patrick Ferguson sent a message to patriots in the countryside along the border between North Carolina and South Carolina, ordering them to cease opposition or suffer the consequences. Fueled with anti-British sentiment, patriots ignored the ultimatum and gathered in force at Sycamore Shoals along the Watauga River in North Carolina.

Learning that the rebels were gathering in large numbers, Lord Cornwallis sent Ferguson to deal with them and to recruit additional Tories for

Death of Major Patrick Ferguson at Kings Mountain.
Courtesy, New York Public Library.

their cause. When Ferguson and his command reached Gilberton, North Carolina, they learned that the enemy was advancing from the north. Ferguson, fearing that the rebels would outnumber him, marched his command south. He soon realized, however, that the rebels, many of whom were mounted, were outpacing him.

Instead of returning to British lines at Charlotte, as he had originally planned, Ferguson decided to make a stand against the rebels at Kings Mountain in South Carolina, a dominant point in a chain of low mountains that straddled the border with North Carolina. After a sixteen-mile march, Ferguson sent his men up Kings Mountain. Although the British force reached the mountain well in advance of the rebels, they neglected to build breastworks or redoubts. This allowed the American force to sneak their way up the pine-covered slope, moving from tree to tree and picking off Ferguson's men with accurate rifle fire. Once they reached the summit, they were able to fire at the Tories without the obstruction of woods.

Ferguson's command, however, was forced to fight in the open and was armed with less accurate smoothbore muskets. They also had the disadvantage of having to fire downhill, which made them overshoot their targets. The Tories relied on the use of volley fire and massed bayonet charges, which were ill suited for the terrain. Although the Tories were successful in pushing the rebels down the hill in three successive bayonet charges, the rebels regrouped after each attack and finally gained the advantage. Ferguson was killed in the battle, and almost his entire command of more than one thousand men was killed, wounded, or captured.

The American victory provided a much-needed tonic to the patriot cause in the South. Because of the defeat, Cornwallis was forced to delay his movement into North Carolina for a year. The battle also caused the Loyalists in the area to think twice about joining the British and swayed neutrals to join the patriots in their fight for independence. Perhaps most significant was the hope that Kings Mountain gave to the patriots, who were still recovering from their humiliating defeats at Camden and Fishing Creek. KENDRA DEBANY

Buchanan, John. *The Road to Guilford Courthouse: The American Revolution in the Carolinas*. New York: Wiley, 1997.

Lumpkin, Henry. *From Savannah to Yorktown: The American Revolution in the South*. Columbia: University of South Carolina Press, 1981.

Messick, Hank. *King's Mountain: The Epic of the Blue Ridge "Mountain Men" in the American Revolution*. Boston: Little, Brown, 1976.

Middlekauf, Robert F. *The Glorious Cause: The American Revolution, 1763–1789*. 2d ed. New York: Oxford University Press, 2005.

LAURENS, HENRY (1724–1792). Merchant, planter, statesman, diplomat. Laurens was born on February 24, 1724, in Charleston, the eldest son of John Laurens, a saddler, and Esther Grasset. Both the Laurens and Grasset families fled France as Huguenot refugees in the 1680s, with John and Esther settling in Charleston about 1715. Henry Laurens provided no details but described his education as "the best . . . which [Charleston] afforded." Following a three-year clerkship in the London countinghouse of James Crokatt, Laurens returned to Charleston in 1747 and formed a commercial partnership with George Austin. Austin & Laurens expanded in 1759 to become Austin, Laurens & (George) Appleby and continued until 1762, when the partnership was dissolved by mutual consent. Laurens subsequently traded on his own. As a merchant, he exported Carolina products (rice, indigo, deerskins, and naval stores) to Britain, Europe, and the West Indies. His vessels returned with wine, textiles, rum, sugar, and slaves. During the early 1760s Laurens's interests expanded to include rice and indigo planting. He owned four South Carolina plantations (Mepkin, Wambaw, Wrights Savannah, and Mount Tacitus), two Georgia plantations (Broughton Island and New Hope), tracts of undeveloped land in both colonies, and town lots

Henry Laurens. Oil on canvas, 1782. Courtesy, National Portrait Gallery, Smithsonian Institution.

in Charleston. The earnings from his mercantile and planting interests made Laurens one of the wealthiest men in America.

Laurens entered public service at an early age, holding local and church offices in Charleston as early as 1751. He first sat in the Commons House of Assembly in 1757, representing St. Philip's Parish. He would be reelected to the colonial or state assemblies seventeen times during his lifetime. He served as a lieutenant in the militia in 1757 and as a lieutenant colonel in the provincial regiment during the Cherokee Expedition of 1761. He refused appointment to the Royal Council in 1764.

During the early stages of the Anglo-American conflict, Laurens gained prominence as a political moderate. On October 23, 1765, at the height of the Stamp Act crisis, a mob invaded his home in search of stamped papers. This incident ended without injury but traumatized his wife and increased the conservative merchant-planter's concern for the rights of individuals threatened by the violence and enthusiasm of the revolution. Between 1767 and 1769 royal officials in South Carolina seized his schooners *Wambaw* and *Broughton Island Packet* and the ship *Ann* for alleged customs violations.

In response Laurens wrote pamphlets explaining his position and castigating the customs and vice-admiralty officials. He also challenged a customs officer to a duel. This aggressive behavior was not uncommon for Laurens, who sought vindication with dueling pistols on at least five occasions during his lifetime.

Laurens's life took a new direction in May 1770 after the death of his wife, Eleanor Ball. Married to Laurens since June 25, 1750, Eleanor had given birth to twelve or thirteen children. Laurens now made the education of his five surviving children, especially his three sons, his foremost life's work. He suspended direct supervision of his planting and commercial interests and sailed to England in September 1771. From there he traveled to the Continent, where he found suitable schools for his two older sons in Geneva, Switzerland. During the time he spent in England, Laurens and several other South Carolinians in London signed petitions to Parliament and the king seeking redress of American grievances.

The South Carolina to which Laurens returned in 1774 had moved beyond peaceful petition to revolution. Within weeks of his landing, St. Philip's Parish elected him to the First Provincial Congress. In June 1775 he became president of the Provincial Congress and the Council of Safety and consequently the state's chief executive during the establishment of the provincial regiments and the transition from royal to independent status. He contributed to South Carolina's first constitution and served as vice president in the first state government formed in March 1776. He remained an active and moderating force in South Carolina's revolutionary movement from 1775 until he left to serve in the Continental Congress in June 1777.

Laurens has been frequently cited by historians as one of the few citizens in the lower South who expressed opposition to slavery in America as early as the 1770s. In an oft-quoted passage from his correspondence, he wrote (after receiving a copy of the Declaration of Independence), "I abhor slavery," despite participating in the slave trade early in his career, owning 298 slaves as late as 1790, and the fact that there is little evidence that he offered freedom to more than a few of his servants. Laurens understood the harm that slavery posed, to both races, and anticipated that it would end in a bloody conflict. His opposition to slavery, however, had little impact on the institution in South Carolina.

Arriving at Philadelphia in July 1777, Laurens quickly established himself as an active and respected member of the Continental Congress. In November 1777 he succeeded John Hancock as president during one of the most trying times in American history. He took the chair at York, Pennsylvania, where Congress met after Philadelphia had fallen to the British the previous September. During his tenure the Continental army spent its winter encampment at Valley Forge and turmoil in Congress and among Continental officers threatened General George Washington's command. Laurens resigned as president in December 1778 but continued to represent South Carolina in Congress until late 1779. In October that year Congress selected him to travel to Holland and secure a loan and an alliance with the Dutch.

Shortly after departing on his Dutch mission, Laurens, his vessel, and most of his papers were taken by a British warship in September 1780. Charged with high treason, he was a prisoner in the Tower of London from October 1780 through December 1781. After obtaining his parole and subsequent freedom, Laurens learned that he had been named to the American commission to negotiate peace with Britain. The fifteen months spent in confinement ruined his health, however, and permitted him to play only a minor role. Along with Benjamin Franklin, John Adams, and John Jay, Laurens signed the preliminary peace treaty in Paris in November 1782. Traveling to England to regain his health, Laurens did not attend the signing of the definitive treaty in Paris in September 1783.

Laurens returned to South Carolina in January 1785 and withdrew from public affairs. Elected as a delegate to both the 1787 Philadelphia constitutional convention and the 1790 South Carolina constitutional convention, he declined to serve in both. The one minor exception occurred in 1788 when he supported the federal Constitution as a delegate to the South Carolina ratification convention. He spent his declining years successfully rebuilding his war-ravaged estate. He died on December 8, 1792, at his Mepkin plantation on the Cooper River. As stipulated in his will, he chose to have his remains cremated before burial. His ashes were interred at Mepkin. C. JAMES TAYLOR

Clark, Peggy J. "Henry Laurens's Role in the Anglo-American Peace Negotiations." Master's thesis, University of South Carolina, 1991.

Frech, Laura Page. "The Career of Henry Laurens in the Continental Congress, 1777–1779." Ph.D. diss., University of North Carolina at Chapel Hill, 1972.

Hamer, Philip M., et al., eds. *The Papers of Henry Laurens.* 16 vols. Columbia: University of South Carolina Press, 1968–2003.

McDonough, Daniel J. *Christopher Gadsden and Henry Laurens: The Parallel Lives of Two American Patriots.* Selinsgrove, Pa.: Susquehanna University Press, 2000.

Moore, Warner Oland. "Henry Laurens: A Charleston Merchant in the Eighteenth Century, 1747–1771." Ph.D. diss., University of Alabama, 1974.

Wallace, David Duncan. *The Life of Henry Laurens.* New York: Putnam, 1915.

LAURENS, JOHN (1754–1782). Soldier, diplomat. Laurens was born in Charleston on October 28, 1754, the son of the prominent merchant and planter Henry Laurens and his wife, Eleanor Ball. After studying under tutors in Charleston, Laurens traveled to London in 1771 for further schooling. He first enrolled in Richard Clarke's school for Carolina boys before moving to Geneva, Switzerland, in May 1772. Laurens lived in Geneva, a city noted for its republicanism and excellence in education, until August 1774, when he returned to London to study law in the Middle Temple at the Inns of Court.

In December 1776 Laurens sailed to Charleston to enlist in the American War of Independence. He left behind in England his pregnant wife, Martha Manning, whom he had secretly married earlier in the year. The following summer he traveled to Philadelphia with his father, who had been elected to the Continental Congress. Laurens joined General George Washington's staff and became the best friend of fellow aide Alexander Hamilton. In the forefront at the battles of Brandywine, Germantown, and Monmouth, Laurens won a reputation for reckless bravery.

After the British shifted military operations to the South, Laurens proposed that South Carolina arm slaves and grant them freedom in return for their military service. In March 1779 Congress approved his idea and commissioned him lieutenant colonel. Elected to the South Carolina House of Representatives, Laurens introduced his black-regiment plan in 1779 and 1780 and met overwhelming defeat each time. His belief that blacks shared a similar nature with whites and could aspire to freedom in a republican society would set Laurens apart from all other prominent South Carolinians in the Revolutionary War period.

At the same time, Laurens continued his military service. When the British threatened Charleston in May 1779, he opposed Governor John Rutledge's offer to surrender the city on the condition that the state be allowed to remain neutral for the duration of the war. That fall Laurens commanded an infantry column in the failed assault on Savannah. After being captured when Charleston surrendered in May 1780, he was exchanged in November.

In December 1780 Congress appointed Laurens special minister to France. He arrived in France in March 1781. In a whirlwind two-month mission he obtained a loan from the Netherlands, military supplies, and French assurances that their navy would operate in American waters that year. Laurens finished his diplomatic duties in time to join Washington at Yorktown, where the timely arrival of the French fleet secured a decisive American victory. Laurens represented the American army in negotiating the British surrender.

Laurens returned to South Carolina and made a final attempt to secure approval of his plan for a black regiment. At Jacksonborough in early 1782, the House again decisively rejected his proposal, though the debate was heated. Laurens served under General Nathanael Greene and spent his final months operating a spy network that gathered intelligence of British activities in Charleston. On August 27, 1782, he was killed in a skirmish on the Combahee River. GREGORY D. MASSEY

Massey, Gregory D. *John Laurens and the American Revolution.* Columbia: University of South Carolina Press, 2000.

LINCOLN, BENJAMIN (1733–1810). Soldier. Lincoln was born in Hingham, Massachusetts, on January 24, 1733, the sixth child of Colonel Benjamin Lincoln and Elizabeth Thaxter. Lincoln rose to prominence in the Seven Years' War, where he gained extensive experience in military planning and organization. A strong supporter of revolutionary activities in Massachusetts, that colony appointed him a major general of militia in February 1776. He served in the campaign around New York in the summer and fall of 1776 and earned Washington's admiration and respect. Acting on Washington's recommendation, the Continental Congress appointed him a major general in the Continental army on February 14, 1777. Later that year he helped Horatio Gates defeat General John Burgoyne's British army in the Saratoga campaign.

Impressed with his abilities, the Continental Congress chose Lincoln to replace Major General Robert Howe as commander of the Southern Department in September 1778. Lincoln arrived in Charleston to take command in December. The British captured Savannah in late December 1778 and in the ensuing months reestablished some control over Georgia. Lincoln's desire to drive the British from Georgia exposed South Carolina to attack and brought the wrath of South Carolinians upon him. In late April 1779 he marched the bulk of his army up the Savannah River and crossed to Augusta, intending to force the British from the Georgia backcountry. General Augustine Prevost, meanwhile, crossed the Savannah and marched his army to Charleston. Lincoln returned to the state, but not before Prevost's troops threatened Charleston and ravaged farms and plantations throughout the Lowcountry. Shortly after Prevost's troops withdrew toward Georgia, Lincoln complained to General William Moultrie, "it appears . . . that I have lost the confidence of the people." Lincoln wished to resign from command of the Southern Department, but Moultrie and Governor John Rutledge convinced him to remain. He led American forces in the disastrous Franco-American effort against Savannah in October 1779.

Lincoln had the misfortune to preside over the single worst defeat of American forces during the Revolutionary War, the loss of Charleston. Probably influenced by his experience in the spring campaign of 1779, Lincoln elected to hold Charleston against a strong army and fleet under General Sir Henry Clinton and Admiral Marriot Arbuthnot. Although several officers recommended evacuation, Lincoln decided to keep his army within his works. The Americans staved off the British for six weeks, but Clinton's force eventually applied overwhelming pressure and the city capitulated on May 12, 1780. Governor Rutledge criticized Lincoln for giving up the town, but other South Carolinians praised his conduct. The historian David Ramsay thought that "great praise" was due Lincoln for "baffling, for three months, the greatly superior force of Sir Henry Clinton and Admiral Arbuthnot." Exchanged in November 1780, Lincoln served as second in command to Washington during the Yorktown campaign, accepting the sword of Cornwallis's second in command at the surrender of Yorktown. He later served as head of the newly created War Department and in various positions in Massachusetts government after the war. Lincoln died in Hingham, Massachusetts, on May 9, 1810. CARL BORICK

Mattern, David B. *Benjamin Lincoln and the American Revolution.* Columbia: University of South Carolina Press, 1995.
Moultrie, William. *Memoirs of the American Revolution.* 1802. Reprint, New York: New York Times, 1968.
Ramsay, David. *History of the Revolution in South Carolina, from a British Province to an Independent State.* 2 vols. Trenton, N.J.: Isaac Collins, 1785.

LOWNDES, RAWLINS (1721–1800). Jurist, governor. Lowndes was born in 1721 on St. Kitts in the West Indies, the son of Charles Lowndes and Ruth Rawlins. In 1730 the family migrated to South Carolina, where Lowndes's extravagant father fell into financial ruin and committed suicide in May 1736. His youngest sons, Charles and Rawlins, became wards of South Carolina's provost marshal Robert Hall. Under Hall's tutelage, Rawlins Lowndes learned the intricacies of South Carolina's legal system. In 1745 Lowndes followed his mentor's footsteps and became provost marshal, the chief law enforcement officer of the colony.

On August, 15, 1748, Lowndes married Amarinthia Elliott, whose dowry brought him a plantation on Stono River in St. Paul's Parish. He now qualified for a seat in the Commons House of Assembly and was elected in 1749. After Amarinthia died in childbirth in January 1750, Lowndes acquired Horseshoe Plantation in St. Bartholomew's Parish and thereafter represented that parish in the assembly for most of the following twenty-five years. He was married two more times: to Mary Cartwright on December 23, 1751 (she died in 1770) and to Sarah Jones from January 1773 until his death. These unions produced seven and three children respectively.

Overburdened by his public and private duties, Lowndes experienced declining health, and he resigned as provost marshal in June 1754. He sailed to England to recover his health, returning to South Carolina in December 1755. After his arrival Lowndes rose to prominence in the Commons House of Assembly and held several important committee assignments. In September 1763 the assembly elected Lowndes to the Speaker's chair, where he defended the assembly's prerogatives against encroachments from royal governors, the upper house, and the ministry in England. A political moderate, Lowndes apparently was not daring enough for his colleagues, who replaced him with Peter Manigault in October 1765.

In February 1766 Lowndes was appointed assistant judge, a position he held for six years, and he took legal positions that won him praise. He argued that South Carolina's courts should be opened, despite the Stamp Act's provision that legal documents bear the required stamps. In 1773 Lowndes ruled that the upper house, or Royal Council, composed of placemen who served at the pleasure of the crown, was not equivalent to the British House of Lords. This argument struck a devastating political blow against the Royal Council's prestige and marked the high point of Lowndes's public career.

In October 1772 Lowndes was again elected Speaker of the Commons House of Assembly, and he retained that post until the dissolution of royal government in 1775. A reluctant revolutionary, Lowndes hoped for an accommodation between the colonies and Britain and reportedly reacted to Thomas Paine's *Common Sense* with a stream of profanities. Nevertheless, he held important posts in the early years of the Revolutionary War, serving in the Provincial Congress and on the Council of Safety. When John Rutledge resigned as president (governor) of South Carolina in March 1778 to protest the proposed state constitution, the legislature elected Lowndes.

Lowndes's brief tenure as president proved frustrating. Perhaps influenced by his long service in the legislative branch, he was reluctant to use the powers of his office. Preferring to keep South Carolina's supplies and militia for state use only, Lowndes did not fully cooperate with Continental army generals Robert Howe and Benjamin Lincoln in their efforts to defend the lower South from British attacks. Lowndes retired to private life in February 1779 and thereafter played no major role in the Revolution.

Lowndes suffered extensive property losses during the British occupation of South Carolina. In late 1780 he petitioned to be restored to the rights of a British subject. Though the South Carolina state legislature did not confiscate Lowndes's property because of this decision, he was stripped of his full citizenship until the summer of 1783.

Lowndes's last major public act occurred while he was representing the city parishes in the S.C. House from 1787 to 1790. In 1788 he argued against ratification of the federal constitution and predicted that the South, as a minority section reliant on slavery, would be at the mercy of northern commercial interests. He was elected to his final public office in 1788, serving one term as intendant (mayor) of Charleston. In his final decade, Lowndes recouped the financial losses he had incurred during the Revolution. After a brief illness, he died in Charleston on August 24, 1800, and was buried in St. Philip's Churchyard. GREGORY D. MASSEY

Vipperman, Carl J. *The Rise of Rawlins Lowndes, 1721–1800.* Columbia: University of South Carolina Press, 1978.

LOYALISTS. Historians have correctly labeled the American Revolution as the nation's first civil war. No greater example of this internecine struggle can be found than in South Carolina, where the Revolution degenerated into a bitter-brothers war that was fought with little compassion or restraint. A leading factor contributing to this inner conflict was the relatively large number of inhabitants who professed a continuing allegiance to the king of Great Britain. The precise extent of Loyalist strength in South Carolina will never be known because many people switched allegiances as circumstances dictated during the protracted war.

Complicating the task of measuring Loyalist sentiment is the difficulty in defining loyalism. The most conspicuous expression of loyalism was the bearing of arms against patriot forces. At least five thousand South Carolinians took up arms against the Whig government during the Revolution. Thousands more Loyalist-leaning Americans helped to cripple the American cause in South Carolina by spying for the British, supplying them with provisions, attacking stores and supplies belonging to Whig authorities, and other acts of resistance.

Perhaps 25 percent of white South Carolinians either actively opposed the movement for independence or supported British authority against the state government during the war. But a far greater number of people resisted the Whig government in subtle but no less debilitating ways, either by refusing to pay their wartime taxes and sell their supplies to the army or by deserting the army as soon as they could and avoiding conscription. Whig leaders saw little distinction between the more ardent Loyalists and the Loyalist-neutrals, those who simply refused to help the patriots unless forced to do so. The Provincial Congress in June 1775 urged all citizens to sign an "Association" as proof of their allegiance to the Whig government and branded any person refusing obedience to its authority as "an enemy to the liberties of America" and subject to patriot vengeance.

Nearly equally troublesome as determining the number of Loyalists in South Carolina is explaining their continued allegiance to the king of Great Britain. Most Loyalists, like the rebels, opposed Parliament's claims to tax America. Unlike the rebels, however, Loyalists doubted that Parliament intended to undermine the colonists' rights as Englishmen. They also thought that separation was illegal and feared that it would lead to a civil war in America.

Other Loyalists sided with the British for more self-serving reasons, particularly crown-appointed officials and former British officers and enlisted men who owed their jobs to the empire and major city merchants who depended on British trade. Loyalists were disproportionately represented among non-English ethnic minorities. In addition, many backcountry settlers opposed the Whig government because of influential local men who cast their lot with Britain, and because their long-standing struggle with the coastal aristocracy for schools, roads, courts, and political representation made them unsympathetic to the patriots' cries of ministerial abuse.

One common element among Loyalists in South Carolina is that nearly all immigrated to the province after 1765 only about one in six was native born. As recent arrivals, they were unlikely to support a movement that was defying the authority from which they had obtained their lands. In short, Loyalists came from every sector of society, with approximately 45 percent comprised of small farmers 30 percent of merchants, artisans, and shopkeepers 15 percent of large farmers and planters and 10 percent of crown officials and professionals.

Loyalist strength in South Carolina varied according to region. It was weakest in the Lowcountry, where the king's friends were greatly outnumbered and where Loyalist leaders failed to organize among themselves and to cultivate public opinion by offering a reasonable alternative to rebellion. Their passive disapproval of Whig measures allowed the patriot party to carry out its revolutionary program there with remarkably little intimidation and violence. However, Whig leaders faced much stronger resistance in the backcountry, where a large party of Loyalists, led by influential men of high intelligence and determination, formed themselves into military units and openly defied Whig measures. To counter resistance there, patriot leaders in Charleston penned and distributed throughout the interior pamphlets explaining the American cause and appointed scores of local leaders to prominent positions in the Whig government and military. Still, large areas of resistance remained in the backcountry.

To confront this serious threat, the Council of Safety in July 1775 appointed William Henry Drayton and William Tennent, both active leaders of the radical faction in the Provincial Congress, as emissaries to the backcountry. Using one-sided arguments, economic coercion, and military threats, Drayton and Tennent convinced some Loyalist leaders in the region to sign a neutrality pact at the village of Ninety Six on September 16. However, other Loyalist leaders, such as Thomas Fletchall, Moses Kirkland, and Robert Cunningham, were upset with Drayton's Machiavellian tactics and raised a large force of king's men (approximately four thousand) to seize Whig munitions in the region and attack their small military outpost at Ninety Six. In response, the Provincial Congress ordered Colonel Richard Richardson to raise an army to crush the backcountry dissidents. In December 1775 Richardson's forces engaged and defeated the Loyalist army at the Great Cane Break near the Cherokee Indian line. This defeat marked the end of Loyalist resistance in the interior until British occupation in 1780.

Despite this defeat at the Great Cane Break, the Loyalist uprising in 1775 had an important effect on British military strategy by convincing English politicians and generals that Loyalists were numerous and pugnacious in the southern backcountry. Thus, when British military efforts faltered in the northern colonies by early 1778, British leaders created a new "southern strategy" to seize key southern ports and, with the aid of Loyalist militiamen, move back toward the north, pacifying one region after another.

The southern strategy succeeded in its earliest stages. The British quickly captured Savannah in December 1778 and occupied Charleston in May 1780 after a lengthy siege. Several hundred South Carolinians, mostly Lowcountry merchants, shopkeepers, and artisans interested in maintaining their business operations, signed the oath of allegiance proffered by the British. However, when British forces moved into the interior to liberate and organize the loyal population, they discovered that the king's friends were not so numerous or as steadfast as they had expected. British officers in South Carolina managed to muster only 2,500 men into eighteen poorly supplied militia regiments. Moreover, excesses committed by the British military and their Loyalist allies in their attempt to conquer the backcountry drove many of the uncommitted into the Whig camp and ignited a virulent and bloody civil war that involved people of all ages and both sexes.

Despite the acrimonious and personal nature of fighting in South Carolina during the last years of the conflict, the victorious Whig government treated the defeated Loyalists with relative leniency. However, approximately 4,200 white Loyalists from the state decided that they could not live under a government independent from the king and emigrated from South Carolina to the British Caribbean, East Florida, England, and Canada. Their property, along with that of Loyalists remaining behind, was subject to confiscation by the General Assembly. At their meeting at Jacksonborough in January–February 1782, legislators considered placing as many as seven hundred people on a "confiscation list." The legislature was quickly flooded with petitions for relief from the confiscation law. The assembly, realizing that it was impractical to punish such a large number of Loyalists, most of whom were natives or long-standing residents of the state who found themselves vulnerable after the fall of Charleston, followed a policy of moderation. In most cases, the assembly removed petitioners from the confiscation list and, instead, fined them 12 percent of the value of their property. Although a few people were upset with the legislature's lenient policy toward the former Loyalists, this policy generally helped to restore the state to a relative degree of harmony by eroding much of the bitterness engendered by the protracted war. KEITH KRAWCZYNSKI

Barnwell, Robert W., Jr. "Loyalism in South Carolina, 1765–1785." Ph.D. diss., Duke University, 1941.

Brown, Wallace. *The King's Friends: The Composition and Motives of the American Loyalist Claimants.* Providence, R.I.: Brown University Press, 1965.

Coker, Kathryn Roe. "The Artisan Loyalists of Charleston, South Carolina." In *Loyalists and Community in North America,* edited by Robert M. Calhoon, Timothy M. Barnes, and George A. Rawlyk. Westport, Conn.: Greenwood, 1994.

Lambert, Robert Stansbury. *South Carolina Loyalists in the American Revolution.* Columbia: University of South Carolina Press, 1987.

Singer, Charles. *South Carolina in the Confederation.* 1941. Reprint, Philadelphia: Porcupine, 1976.

LYNCH, THOMAS, JR. (1749–1779). Signer of the Declaration of Independence. Born on August 5, 1749, in Prince George Winyah Parish, Lynch was the only son of Thomas Lynch, Sr. (ca. 1727–1776), and Elizabeth Allston. He attended the Indigo Society School in Georgetown and then traveled to

England to pursue his education. There, he enrolled at Eton and then Caius College, Cambridge. Lynch also read law at the Middle Temple in London.

After his return to South Carolina in 1772, Lynch abandoned law to become a planter at Peach Tree Plantation in St. James Santee Parish. On May 14, 1772, he married Elizabeth Shubrick, daughter of Thomas Shubrick and Sarah Motte. At his father's urging, Lynch soon thereafter entered public life. He served in the First and Second Provincial Congresses of South Carolina (1774–1776), on the constitutional committee of South Carolina (1776), and in the first General Assembly (1776). In June 1775 Lynch received a commission as captain in the First South Carolina Regiment. While recruiting in North Carolina in July 1775, Lynch contracted a fever that left him in poor health for the remainder of his brief life. With his company he served at Fort Johnson from September 1775 until his election to the Second Continental Congress in March 1776.

Lynch's father had been elected to the First Continental Congress in 1774 but suffered a stroke in early 1776 that left him unable to perform his public duties. The younger Lynch joined his father in Philadelphia and presented his credentials to Congress on April 24. Only twenty-six years old and the second-youngest member of Congress, Thomas Lynch, Jr., was the fifty-second signer of the Declaration of Independence. His father was too ill to sign. Thomas Jr.'s own poor health precluded his continued service in the Congress. Together, father and son left Philadelphia in December 1776 to return to South Carolina, but the senior Lynch died during the trip.

In ill health, Thomas Lynch, Jr., retired to his plantation. He represented St. James Santee Parish in the second (1776–1778) General Assembly. He was reelected in 1779, but his declining health prevented him from completing his full term. On December 17, 1779, in an attempt to regain his health, Lynch and his wife set sail for the south of France. Their ship was lost at sea en route to the West Indies. ALEXIA JONES HELSLEY

Bailey, N. Louise, and Elizabeth Ivey Cooper, eds. *Biographical Directory of the South Carolina House of Representatives.* Vol. 3, *1775–1790.* Columbia: University of South Carolina Press, 1981.

Horne, Paul A., Jr. "Forgotten Leaders: South Carolina's Delegation to the Continental Congress, 1774–1789." Ph.D. diss., University of South Carolina, 1988.

LYNCH, THOMAS, SR. (ca. 1727–1776). Legislator, delegate to Continental Congress. Lynch was born in St. James Santee Parish, the son of Thomas Lynch and Sabina Vanderhorst. His father became a wealthy rice planter with several plantations along the Santee River. Lynch's first marriage, in 1745 to Elizabeth Allston, produced three children. On March 6, 1755, Lynch married Hannah Motte, daughter of Jacob Motte and Elizabeth Martin. His second marriage produced one daughter.

A prominent planter, Lynch was active in public affairs. He was the first president of the Winyah Indigo Society (1755–1757) and represented Prince Frederick Parish (1752–1754, 1757–1760), St. James Santee Parish (1754–1757), and Prince George Winyah Parish (1760–1775) in the Commons House of Assembly. Visiting Charleston in early 1773, the Massachusetts lawyer and patriot Josiah Quincy described Lynch in the Commons House as "a man of sense, and a patriot."

From an early date, Lynch opposed efforts by the British to encroach upon colonial autonomy. He was a delegate to the Stamp Act Congress of 1765 in New York and was a member of the Non-Importation Association (1769), serving on its General Committee. As one of South Carolina's best-known and most ardent patriots, Lynch became a great favorite of the Charleston Sons of Liberty. In 1774 Lynch was elected a delegate to the First Continental Congress (1774–1775) in Philadelphia, and he was reelected to the Second Continental Congress (1776). In Congress, Lynch played an active role in the proceedings and earned the respect of his fellow delegates for his "plain, sensible" manner. Silas Deane, a delegate from Connecticut, recorded that Lynch "wears his hair strait, his clothes in the plainest order, and is highly esteemed." Lynch was also elected by St. James Santee Parish to the Second Provincial Congress (1775–1776) and the first South Carolina General Assembly (1776), although he did not participate in either assembly.

While attending Congress in early 1776, Lynch suffered a stroke that left him paralyzed and unable to participate in legislative affairs. In 1776 the South Carolina Provincial Congress elected his son Thomas Lynch, Jr., as a delegate to the Continental Congress in order to assist his father. Although still a delegate, the senior Lynch's declining health prevented him from signing the Declaration of Independence, leaving a gap between the signatures of Edward Rutledge and Thomas Heyward, Jr. However, Thomas Jr. was among the signers.

In December 1776 Lynch left Philadelphia with his son to return to South Carolina. En route, he suffered a second stroke and died in Annapolis, Maryland, where he was buried in St. Anne's Churchyard. ALEXIA JONES HELSLEY

Edgar, Walter, and N. Louise Bailey, eds. *Biographical Directory of the South Carolina House of Representatives*. Vol. 2, *The Commons House of Assembly, 1692–1775*. Columbia: University of South Carolina Press, 1977.

Horne, Paul A., Jr. "Forgotten Leaders: South Carolina's Delegation to the Continental Congress, 1774–1789." Ph.D. diss., University of South Carolina, 1988.

Weir, Robert M. *Colonial South Carolina: A History.* 1983. Reprint, Columbia: University of South Carolina Press, 1997.

MAHAM, HEZEKIAH (1739–1789). Soldier, legislator. Born on June 26, 1739, Hezekiah Maham achieved the status of a successful planter in St. Stephen's Parish by 1772. He represented that parish in the Second Provincial Congress at the onset of the Revolutionary War, but it would be through his military service that he would gain distinction. While the details of his early service remain unclear, in records Maham first appears at the head of a volunteer company of militia early in 1776 and is later promoted to the rank of major in a state regiment of light dragoons in 1779. After the fall of Charleston in May 1780, Maham joined Francis Marion's partisan corps and served as a principal commander of cavalry in Marion's brigade.

In the spring of 1781, Marion's partisan band joined with the Continentals of Henry Lee's Legion and marched on Fort Watson, a key British post between Charleston and the backcountry. The garrison was strategically located at the top of an ancient Indian mound, making a conventional assault suicidal. Major Maham suggested that a log tower be assembled with a platform high enough to allow riflemen to fire into the fort. The structure was completed on the morning of April 23, and an American assault party, protected by suppressing rifle fire from the tower, forced the garrison commander to surrender. Though not a new idea to siege warfare, the Maham Tower (as it would come to be known) was effective and would be used by patriot forces at the sieges of Augusta and Ninety Six later in the year.

On June 21, 1781, Maham was promoted to the rank of lieutenant colonel and appointed to command a battalion of light dragoons, which would come to be known as Maham's Legion. The appointment of Peter Horry to raise a similar corps eventually led to a quarrel between the two officers over rank. Nonetheless, Maham led his unit in a crucial assault at the Battle of Quinby Bridge on July 17, 1781. Later, in mid-November, Maham led a raid on a British hospital at Fairlawn Plantation that yielded some one hundred prisoners. In March 1782 the two cavalry units of Horry and Maham were combined under Maham's command. However, he took ill shortly afterward and withdrew to his plantation, where he was promptly captured and paroled by Tories.

Known for his temper, Maham once forced a deputy sheriff to eat and swallow a summons the latter was trying to serve on him. Elected to several terms in the South Carolina General Assembly during and after the Revolution, both as a representative and a senator, Maham also held sundry offices for the parish of St. Stephen's. He married twice. His first wife was Anne Guerin his second was Mary Palmer. The marriages produced two daughters. Maham died on his plantation sometime between April 4, 1789, when he wrote his will, and June 1, 1789. SAMUEL K. FORE

Lumpkin, Henry. *From Savannah to Yorktown: The American Revolution in the South.* Columbia: University of South Carolina Press, 1981.

Rankin, Hugh F. *Francis Marion: The Swamp Fox.* New York: Crowell, 1973.

Stevens, Michael E. "Wealth, Influence or Powerful Connections: Aedanus Burke and the Case of Hezekiah Maham." *South Carolina Historical Magazine* 81 (April 1980): 163–68.

Weller, Jac. "Irregular but Effective: Partizan Weapons Tactics in the American Revolution, Southern Theatre." *Military Affairs* 21 (autumn 1957): 118–31.

MANIGAULT, GABRIEL (1704–1781). Merchant, legislator. Manigault was born on April 21, 1704, in Charleston, the son of Pierre Manigault and Judith Giton. His parents were refugees who fled France after the revocation of the Edict of Nantes. Throughout his life he remained a member of the French Protestant Church in Charleston, but he also owned a pew and worshiped at St. Philip's Church. He married Ann Ashby on April 29, 1730. The marriage produced one son, Peter, who would become a leading figure in the Commons House of Assembly.

Manigault rose from modest origins to become the leading merchant and private banker of colonial South Carolina. He operated retail shops on Tradd Street selling imported wine, fabrics, and dry goods. He also owned several trading vessels, in which he exported rice, naval stores, and other domestic products. Lacking family and business ties with Britain, he traded principally with the West Indies, Philadelphia, and New York. Known to disapprove of the slave trade, Manigault was reluctant to lend money to slave dealers. On a few occasions, however, he did finance the importation of slave cargoes, and at his death he owned nearly three hundred slaves. In his business dealings and personal affairs, he was known as an honest, fair, and benevolent man. He eschewed business partnerships, preferring to conduct business by himself. In addition to trade, Manigault acquired extensive real estate holdings in Charleston and the surrounding area, including Mount Pleasant plantation (from which the present city takes its name) and Silk Hope plantation, where he experimented with silk cultivation and wine production. By the time he retired from business life in 1767, he had amassed a large fortune.

Manigault was an active member and officer of the Charleston Library Society, and for many years he housed that society's collection and its librarian in one of his tenements. He was also a valued member of the South Carolina Society, to which he left a legacy of £5,000 sterling to fund that society's primary school. During his civic career Manigault acted as a commissioner of public bodies, representing such matters as free schools, streets, markets, bills of credit, ferries, and the Indian trade. Between 1733 and 1754 he served in the Commons House of Assembly, representing first the parish of St. Philip's and later St. Thomas and St. Denis Parish. He held the office of public treasurer of the province from 1735 until 1743, and the accuracy of his accounts contributed to the stability of South Carolina during these difficult years. Manigault was twice recommended by Lieutenant Governor William Bull to a place on the Royal Council, but he declined both offers. His sentiments were with the mechanics of Charleston, who would eventually argue for separation from the British crown.

Although Manigault sought to tread a conservative path in the movement toward American independence, he was also South Carolina's principal Revolutionary War financier. Between 1776 and 1779 he lent the nascent state government a total of £652,500 (South Carolina currency), a sum far greater than was lent by any other individual. After the capitulation of Charleston to the British army in May 1780, Manigault spent his last days on his plantation in Goose Creek. He died on June 5, 1781, and was buried in St. Philip's Parish. NICHOLAS MICHAEL BUTLER

Crouse, Maurice A. "Gabriel Manigault: Charleston Merchant." *South Carolina Historical Magazine* 68 (October 1967): 220–31.

Edgar, Walter, and N. Louise Bailey, eds. *Biographical Directory of the South Carolina House of Representatives.* Vol. 2, *The Commons House of Assembly, 1692–1775.* Columbia: University of South Carolina Press, 1977.

Manigault Family. Papers. South Carolina Historical Society, Charleston.

MARION, FRANCIS (ca. 1732–1795). Soldier. Marion, of Huguenot descent, was born in St. John's Berkeley Parish, the youngest of six children born to Gabriel Marion and Esther Cordes. A planter, Marion in 1773 built his home, Pond Bluff, about four miles south of Eutaw Springs, a site now beneath the waters of Lake Marion. He commenced his military career in the parish militia in 1756 and joined the campaigns against the Cherokees (1759–1761), rising to the rank of first lieutenant. Having served in local offices, he was elected in 1775 to the First Provincial Congress. Commissioned a captain in the state's Second Regiment in June, he participated in the capture of Fort

Johnson in September. As a major, Marion distinguished himself at the Battle of Sullivan's Island (June 1776), after which he was commissioned a lieutenant colonel in the Continental army. Marion commanded the Second Regiment at the disastrous Franco-American attack on Savannah in autumn 1779. Away on sick leave due to an accident, he eluded capture when Charleston fell to the British in May 1780. Escaping to North Carolina, he and a small party linked up with Horatio Gates's army preparing for an invasion of South Carolina. Detailed to destroy enemy communication lines, Marion was not present for Gates's defeat at Camden in August.

With a militia commission as brigadier general, Marion organized a partisan force in the Pee Dee region. Between August and December 1780, in an otherwise dismal period for America, Marion gained national recognition for his actions at Great Savannah (August 20), Blue Savannah (September 4), Black Mingo (September 29), Tearcoat Swamp (October 26), Georgetown (November 15), and Halfway Swamp (December 12–13). While some counts place the number of "Marion's Men" at more than two thousand, his band generally consisted of considerably fewer than that and included Continentals. Marion's nickname, the "Swamp Fox," reportedly came from the infamous British officer Banastre Tarleton, who, unable to snare Marion, called him a "damned old fox" and swore that "the devil himself could not catch him." Marion's small-scale hit-and-run tactics disrupted supply lines, intercepted communications, and hampered the enemy considerably. Conditions improved by the spring of 1781, when Marion became a vital part of General Nathanael Greene's combined operations in South Carolina. In 1781 Marion's troops participated in the battles at Fort Watson (April 23), Fort Motte (May 12), Quinby Bridge (July 17), Parker's Ferry (August 13), and Eutaw Springs (September 8). His numerous command problems included Greene's distrust of the militia, his need for Marion's essential horses, an ongoing conflict over rank and command with General Thomas Sumter, and a feud between his subordinates Peter Horry and Hezekiah Maham. This latter feud came to a head while Marion was serving as a senator in the General Assembly at Jacksonborough and resulted in a defeat at the hands of the British at Wambaw Bridge in February 1782. Returning to command, Marion's brigade saw its last engagement at Wadboo Creek in the summer of 1782. Throughout the war, which in South Carolina was a brutally vicious civil conflict, Marion was said to be "humain and Mercifull" but was also known as a severe disciplinarian. Although small in stature, with knees and ankles "badly formed," Marion inspired great loyalty in his ill-clothed, ill-fed, and ill-equipped band.

After the war a penniless Marion, whose plantation had been ruined, was awarded a gold medal, a full Continental colonelcy, and command of Fort Johnson in Charleston harbor. He served in the S.C. Senate in 1783–1786, 1791, and 1792–1794 and was elected to the 1790 state constitutional convention. He continued as a brigadier general in the militia until his retirement in 1794. His finances improved when he married his cousin Mary Esther Videau on April 20, 1786. The union produced no children, but in less than a decade Marion's fortune grew dramatically. Near the end of his life he owned upward of eighteen hundred acres and seventy-three slaves. He died at Pond Bluff on February 27, 1795, and was buried in the family plot at Belle Isle in St. Stephen's Parish. His tomb escaped flooding by the Santee-Cooper project and serves today as a humble monument to the Swamp Fox. His comrade Peter Horry attempted to write a history of Marion's brigade, but it was hopelessly mangled by Mason Locke "Parson" Weems, the first of many to take enormous liberties with Marion's legend. ROY TALBERT, JR.

Bass, Robert. *Swamp Fox: The Life and Campaigns of General Francis Marion.* New York: Holt, 1959.

Rankin, Hugh F. *Francis Marion: The Swamp Fox.* New York: Crowell, 1973.

Simms, William Gilmore. *The Life of Francis Marion.* 1844. Reprint, Freeport, N.Y.: Books for Libraries, 1971.

MATHEWS, JOHN (1744–1802). Governor. Mathews was born in Charleston in 1744, the only son of John Mathews and Sarah Gibbes. In 1764 he began the study of law at the Middle Temple in London. Shortly thereafter he returned to South Carolina, where he clerked for Charles Pinckney before his admission to the bar in 1766. Later that year he married Mary Wragg. They had one son.

Mathews entered public service in 1767, when St. Helena's Parish elected him to the Commons House of Assembly. St. John's Colleton Parish returned Mathews in 1772, but he did not become a legislative mainstay until elected to the First and Second Provincial Congresses in 1775 by St. George's Dorchester Parish. Between 1776 and 1790 Mathews served in the first eight General Assemblies, representing at different times St. George's Dorchester Parish and the Charleston parishes of St. Philip's and St. Michael's. Mathews was chosen the first Speaker of the House of Representatives under the constitution of 1778 but left the position after being elected a delegate to the Continental Congress. He was reelected to additional terms in 1779 and 1780.

As a delegate, Mathews served on several important committees, including as chairman of the Committee at Headquarters, which worked closely with General George Washington to supply and organize the army. Mathews was instrumental in securing the appointment of Nathanael Greene as commander of the Southern Department of the Continental army in December 1780. He also thwarted efforts to sacrifice South Carolina and Georgia to gain independence for the other colonies.

Mathews left Congress in December 1781 and returned home. He attended the legislative session at Jacksonborough, where he was elected governor on January 29, 1782. Mathews faced several serious problems: the state was economically devastated; the Continental army in South Carolina was in disrepair; and the British controlled Charleston. Furthermore, the legislature sought to confiscate Loyalist property, a move with which Mathews disagreed. He started the work of reconstructing South Carolina with a census of the state, necessary for future taxation. To augment white troops available for combat, he favored raising a noncombat corps of African laborers, but the measure was rejected by the General Assembly. Finally, on December 14, 1782, Mathews presided over the reoccupation of Charleston by American forces, ending the British threat to South Carolina.

Mathews was succeeded as governor by Benjamin Guerard on February 4, 1783. Mathews's one year in office was the shortest full term of any South Carolina governor. He remained active in the legislature during the 1780s, and in 1784 he was elected as chancellor of the court of chancery. He served on that court and the court of law and equity until 1797. He served as a trustee of the College of Charleston and helped found the St. George's Club, which encouraged the breeding of good horses. In 1799, following the death of his first wife, he married Sarah Rutledge, sister of John and Edward Rutledge. Mathews died in Charleston on October 26, 1802. PAUL A. HORNE, JR.

Horne, Paul A., Jr. "Forgotten Leaders: South Carolina's Delegation to the Continental Congress, 1774–1789." Ph.D. diss., University of South Carolina, 1988.

——. "The Governorship of John Mathews, 1782–1783." Master's thesis, University of South Carolina, 1982.

Nadelhaft, Jerome J. *The Disorders of War: The Revolution in South Carolina.* Orono: University of Maine Press, 1981.

MCCALL, JAMES (1741–1781). Soldier. McCall was born on August 11, 1741, on Canacocheque Creek in Pennsylvania. He moved southward with his family in his youth, settling first in western Virginia and, after being driven out by Indians, later in Mecklenburg District, North Carolina. A young James McCall appeared in the ranks of a militia company with his father in 1766 and became active during the North Carolina Regulator insurrection. In the early 1770s he moved to the Long Cane District of South Carolina to settle among his Calhoun relatives.

At the onset of the Revolutionary War, McCall was selected as commander of one of three companies of patriot militia formed in the Long Cane area. He commanded his company in the stand against the Loyalists at Ninety Six in November 1775 and was selected the following summer to command a detachment in a covert mission to capture a party of Tories in the Cherokee country. Advancing carefully, McCall's expedition was ambushed by a larger force of Indians. He and six companions were held captive, but McCall alone managed to escape several weeks later.

As the militia gained more structure in the backcountry, McCall was promoted to major of the Upper Ninety Six District Regiment, commanded by his friend and neighbor Andrew Pickens, and he later participated in the decisive battle at Kettle Creek on February 14, 1779. After the fall of Charleston in May 1780, McCall refused to accept parole and retreated into Georgia to continue operations against the crown with Elijah Clark. Undoubtedly he was one of the more active field commanders in South Carolina, as he participated in the actions at Musgrove's Mill, Augusta, King's Mountain, Fish Dam Ford, Blackstock's Plantation, and Long Cane Creek in the turbulent latter half of 1780.

With Andrew Pickens back in command in late December 1780, McCall was appointed to raise a regiment of dragoons and promoted to the rank of lieutenant colonel. The patriot militia of Ninety Six moved to join Brigadier General Daniel Morgan's camp on the Pacolet River in late December 1780, and McCall's new command was immediately attached to the reduced ranks of Lieutenant Colonel William Washington's corps of light horse to pursue a marauding band of Tories. Washington and McCall caught up with the Tories at Hammond's Old Store and inflicted many casualties on the fleeing band. McCall's regiment formed the reserve under Washington and fought well in the signal victory over Tarleton's forces at Cowpens on January 17, 1781. Retreating into North Carolina before Lord Cornwallis's advance, McCall's contingent operated as an important shielding force for the main Continental army. He returned to South Carolina in early March. While coordinating an offensive on the British outpost at Ninety Six, he died from the effects of a wound and smallpox in April 1781. SAMUEL K. FORE

Lumpkin, Henry. *From Savannah to Yorktown: The American Revolution in the South.* Columbia: University of South Carolina Press, 1981.

McCall, Hugh. *History of Georgia: Containing Brief Sketches of the Most Remarkable Events, Up to the Present* Day. 2 vols. Savannah, Ga.: Seymour & Williams, 1811–1816.

Waring, Alice Noble. *The Fighting Elder: Andrew Pickens (1739–1817)*. Columbia: University of South Carolina Press, 1962.

MIDDLETON, ARTHUR (1742–1787). Legislator, signer of the Declaration of Independence. Middleton was born on June 26, 1742, at Middleton Place on the Ashley River in St. Andrew's Parish. He was the son of Henry Middleton and Mary Williams. At age twelve, he was sent to England to complete his education, attending Hackney Academy, Westminster School, and St. John's College (Cambridge) before entering the Middle Temple in London for legal training in 1757. He returned to South Carolina in December 1763. On August 19, 1764, Middleton married the wealthy heiress Mary Izard, daughter of Walter Izard, Jr. The marriage produced nine children.

Possessing financial independence and a civic spirit, Middleton pursued public office. In October 1765 he won a seat in the Commons House of Assembly, where he represented St. Helena's Parish until May 1768. That year he and his wife left for Europe to spend the next three years traveling throughout the Continent studying literature and the fine arts. When Middleton returned to South Carolina in 1771, he avoided political service to oversee his expanding Lowcountry rice plantations and his stable of thoroughbreds. However, as the Anglo-American conflict reached the critical stage in 1775, his strong devotion to American rights motivated him to serve in the assembly and on many revolutionary committees.

Middleton soon emerged as a leader within the extreme faction of the local "patriot party" by organizing and leading raids on the royal armories, raising money for the American cause, planning for the defense of Charleston, encouraging attacks against vocal Loyalists, and proposing the confiscation of property belonging to those who had fled the province. Middleton's enthusiasm earned him a position on the panel drafting South Carolina's first constitution in February 1776 and election as a delegate to the Continental Congress in Philadelphia. There, Middleton, fearful of a British attack on his home state, reluctantly signed the Declaration of Independence. During the next two years Middleton helped frame the Articles of Confederation and desperately tried to get greater military assistance from Congress for the lower South. His failure in this latter goal and the counterproductive dissension in the national assembly encouraged Middleton to return to South Carolina, where he felt he could better serve the American cause.

In March 1778 the General Assembly elected Middleton governor under the state's new constitution. However, Middleton refused the honor, partly because he objected to the democratic trends of the 1778 charter and partly because he hoped for some reconciliation with Great Britain given the lack of concern demonstrated by Congress for southern military needs. Still, Middleton provided valuable assistance in the General Assembly until the siege of Charleston in 1780, when he joined the state militia to help defend the capital. When the city fell to the British on May 12, Middleton was captured and sent to St. Augustine as a prisoner of war. In July 1781 he was exchanged and returned to Philadelphia as a delegate to the Continental Congress, where he promoted South Carolina's commercial interests and pushed for the execution of British general Lord Cornwallis.

After his return to South Carolina in 1783, Middleton devoted his energies to repairing his war-ravaged estate. He returned to the General Assembly in 1785 as a representative from St. George's Dorchester Parish and also served as a trustee of the College of Charleston. Middleton died from an unknown fever on January 1, 1787, and was buried in the family mausoleum at Middleton Place. KEITH KRAWCZYNSKI

Edgar, Walter, and N. Louise Bailey, eds. *Biographical Directory of the South Carolina House of Representatives.* Vol. 2, *The Commons House of Assembly, 1692–1775.* Columbia: University of South Carolina Press, 1977.

Horne, Paul A., Jr. "Forgotten Leaders: South Carolina's Delegation to the Continental Congress, 1774–1789." Ph.D. diss., University of South Carolina, 1988.

Lane, George W. "The Middletons of Eighteenth-Century South Carolina: A Colonial Dynasty, 1678–1787." Ph.D. diss., Emory University, 1990.

MIDDLETON, HENRY (1717–1784). Planter, politician, president of Continental Congress. The son of Arthur Middleton and Sarah Amory, Middleton was born at The Oaks, his father's plantation in St. James Goose Creek Parish. Upon his father's death in 1737, Middleton inherited property in South Carolina, England, and Barbados. Judicious investments and marriages increased his landholdings to nearly twenty plantations totaling fifty thousand acres and about eight hundred slaves. In 1741 Middleton married Mary Williams. The union produced twelve children. Mary also brought him an estate on the Ashley River, which became known as Middleton Place. In 1762, a year after Mary's death, Middleton married Mary Henrietta Bull, daughter of William Bull, the colony's lieutenant governor. In January 1776, four years after Mary's death, Middleton married Lady Mary Mackenzie, daughter of the third earl of Cromartie. The last two marriages produced no children but brought Middleton connections to the royal government and British aristocracy, and perhaps explain his conflicted political stances during the revolutionary period.

In the 1740s and 1750s Middleton served intermittently in the Commons House of Assembly, where he represented St. George's Dorchester Parish. He presided as Speaker of the assembly in 1747 and again from 1754 to 1755. In 1755 he was appointed to the Royal Council. Middleton's position on the council entailed a balancing act. Dissenting against the majority, he voted to open the port of Charleston during the Stamp Act crisis of 1765. In 1769, on the other hand, he joined the rest of the council in opposing the assembly's gift to support John Wilkes. In September 1770 he resigned from the Royal Council, and he thereafter was aligned with the revolutionary movement.

His most important contribution to the Revolution began in July 1774, when he was elected to the First Continental Congress. On October 22 Middleton replaced Peyton Randolph of Virginia as president and presided over Congress until it adjourned on October 26. While president, he signed a "Declaration of Rights and Grievances" that was presented to King George III. Reelected in January 1775, Middleton served in the Second Continental Congress from May to November 1775. During this session Congress organized the Continental army and approved an invasion of Canada, moves that foreshadowed the final break with Great Britain. Perhaps it was no coincidence that Middleton, who preferred to moderate any steps toward independence, refused further service in Congress. Resigning on February 16, 1776, Middleton gave way to his son Arthur, a far more outspoken and radical delegate. Thus it was Arthur, and not his father, who would affix his signature to the Declaration of Independence.

Back in South Carolina, Middleton served in the First and Second Provincial Congresses (1775–1776) and sat on the Council of Safety. Between 1776 and 1778 he served on the Legislative Council (the predecessor of the state Senate) and was twice elected to the state House of Representatives from the city parishes of St. Philip's and St. Michael's. Under the state's 1778 constitution, he was elected to the Senate. When the British captured Charleston in 1780, Middleton took the protection of the crown. Despite this action, he incurred no penalty after the war, probably because his contemporaries remembered his political service and his generosity in lending more than £100,000 to the state. Middleton died in Charleston on June 13, 1784. He was buried in the chancel of the St. James Goose Creek Parish church. GREGORY D. MASSEY

Cheves, Langdon. "Middleton of South Carolina." *South Carolina Historical and Genealogical Magazine* 1 (July 1900): 228–62.

Edgar, Walter, and N. Louise Bailey. *Biographical Directory of the South Carolina House of Representatives*. Vol. 2, *The Commons House of Assembly, 1692–1775*. Columbia: University of South Carolina Press, 1977.

McCrady, Edward. *The History of South Carolina in the Revolution, 1775–1780*. New York: Macmillan, 1901.

MOTTE, REBECCA BREWTON (1737–1815). Revolutionary War heroine. Motte was born on June 15, 1737, at the Santee River plantation of her parents, Robert Brewton and Mary Loughton. She was the sister of Miles Brewton, a leading Charleston merchant. On June 28, 1758, she married Jacob Motte, Jr. (1729–1780), son of the public treasurer of South Carolina, Jacob Motte, Sr. The couple had seven children, but only three daughters survived to adulthood.

Rebecca Motte and Francis Marion, May 1781. Cecil Hartley, The Life of Francis Marion. Courtesy, South Caroliniana Library, University Of South Carolina.

The Mottes actively supported the patriot cause. They supplied food for the soldiers and their animals from their plantation, Mount Joseph, in St. Matthew's Parish, near the junction of the Congaree and Wateree Rivers and McCord's Ferry. This advantageous location, however, overlooked a key British supply route. British troops under the command of an officer named

McPherson took the Motte house and renamed it Fort Motte. They then dug a trench and built a dirt wall to protect the house from patriot attack. The British moved Motte and her household to an outbuilding.

In May 1781 patriot commanders Francis Marion and Henry Lee decided that they would have to burn the house to get the British outpost to surrender. Rebecca Motte gave her consent to the plan and even provided the arrows used to set fire to the roof. The British surrendered after the roof caught fire, and then troops from both sides put out the fire to save the house. Motte reportedly fed all the officers, British and patriot, following the battle.

Motte was connected by the marriages of her daughters to some of the most prominent families in South Carolina, including the Pinckneys, Middletons, and Alstons. Motte died on January 10, 1815, and was buried in the cemetery of St. Philip's Church, Charleston. BRENDA THOMPSON SCHOOLFIELD

Bodie, Idella. *South Carolina Women.* Orangeburg, S.C.: Sandlapper, 1991.

Garden, Alexander. *Anecdotes of the Revolutionary War.* 1822. Reprint, Spartanburg, S.C.: Reprint Company, 1972.

Harkness, David James. "Heroines of the American Revolution." *University of Tennessee Newsletter* 60 (February 1961): 1–16.

Helsley, Alexia Jones. *South Carolinians in the War for American Independence.* Columbia: South Carolina Department of Archives and History, 2000.

Tablet to Mrs. Rebecca Motte, Erected by Rebecca Motte Chapter of the Daughters of the American Revolution, Ceremony of Unveiling at St. Philip's Church, Charleston, S.C., May 9th, 1903. Charleston, S.C.: Dagett, 1903.

MOULTRIE, WILLIAM (1730–1805). Soldier, governor. Moultrie was born in Charleston on November 23, 1730, the son of physician John Moultrie and Lucretia Cooper. He married Damaris Elizabeth de St. Julien on December 10, 1749, and acquired a large plantation in St. John's Berkeley Parish, where he resided. Three children were born to this union, one dying in infancy. Moultrie later married Hannah Motte Lynch, the widow of Thomas Lynch, in October 1779. They had no children.

In 1752, at the age of twenty-one, Moultrie won election to the Commons House of Assembly from St. John's Berkeley Parish. Over the next four decades Moultrie was a fixture in South Carolina government, representing various Lowcountry parishes in royal, revolutionary, and state assemblies almost continually until his retirement from public office in 1794. Equally active in the military, Moultrie served in campaigns against the Cherokees in 1759 and 1760–1761, and attained the rank of colonel of militia by 1774. When the Revolutionary War began the following year, the Second Provincial Congress elected Moultrie as colonel of the Second South Carolina Regiment of

General William Moultrie (1739–1805), by Rembrandt Peale. Oil on canvas. Courtesy, National Portrait Gallery, Smithsonian Institution.

Foot. He also designed what has been called the first American battle flag: an indigo blue field with a white crescent in the upper left corner and possibly the word "Liberty" stitched in the center.

Moultrie achieved national fame on June 28, 1776, when he successfully defended Fort Sullivan against a British attack and saved Charleston from capture. Other units contributed to the defense, but it was the famous palmetto-log and sand fort and Moultrie's command of four hundred men and thirty cannons that became forever associated with the victory. Moultrie became an instant hero, thanked by Congress, and the fort was renamed Fort Moultrie in his honor. Soon thereafter, when his regiment became part of the Continental Line, Moultrie was promoted to brigadier general. Moultrie enjoyed further success later in the war. In February 1779, at the Battle of Port Royal Island, Moultrie dislodged the British from the Beaufort region. The following May he saved Charleston again by skillfully delaying a British advance up the coast from Savannah. However, when the British returned to South Carolina the following year, another successful defense of Charleston proved impossible. Serving as second in command to General Benjamin Lincoln, Moultrie vigorously opposed the city's surrender. After Charleston fell in May 1780, Moultrie was imprisoned at Haddrell's Point and later was sent to Philadelphia, where he was exchanged in early 1782. Returning to active duty, Moultrie held the rank of major general at the end of the war.

Resuming a role in politics, Moultrie returned to the General Assembly in 1783. Two years later, on May 10, 1785, he was elected governor. He served until 1787, during which time his legislative and military experience helped greatly in dealing with difficult postwar issues: establishing the state's credit, reorganizing the militia, improving internal navigation, managing the exodus of banished Tories, creating a county court system, and relocating the state capital from Charleston to Columbia. After additional service in the state Senate, Moultrie began a second tenure in the governor's chair in 1792. It proved to be a tumultuous term. Alexander Moultrie, his half brother and longtime state attorney general, was impeached for financial misconduct in 1792. The governor drew fire for his public support of the French Revolution and its emissary in Charleston, Edmond Genêt, who had attempted to license privateers and recruit volunteers to retake Louisiana from Spain for France. Criticism from state legislators and the Washington administration ended Genêt's efforts and forced Moultrie to issue a proclamation forbidding South Carolinians from enlisting in such expeditions.

Leaving office in 1794, Moultrie retired to his plantation in St. John's Berkeley Parish. Aside from political and military service, Moultrie was actively involved in various organizations. He participated in the South Carolina Society and the St. Andrew's Society for nearly fifty years. He helped found the South Carolina Jockey Club in 1758 and the Washington Race Course in Charleston in 1792. In addition, Moultrie served as president of the state Society of the Cincinnati from its inception in 1783 until his death. In 1802 Moultrie published his *Memoirs of the American Revolution*, which remains a classic source on the war. He died in Charleston on September 27, 1805. ROY TALBERT, JR.

Bailey, N. Louise, Mary L. Morgan, and Carolyn R. Taylor, eds. *Biographical Directory of the South Carolina Senate, 1776–1985.* 3 vols. Columbia: University of South Carolina Press, 1986.

Klein, Rachel N. *Unification of a Slave State: The Rise of the Planter Class in the South Carolina Backcountry, 1760–1808.* Chapel Hill: University of North Carolina Press, 1990.

Moultrie, William. *Memoirs of the American Revolution.* 1802. Reprint, New York: New York Times, 1968.

Nadelhaft, Jerome J. *The Disorders of War: The Revolution in South Carolina.* Orono: University of Maine Press, 1981.

MOULTRIE FLAG. In January 1776 the South Carolina Council of Safety delivered twenty-three yards of blue cloth to Colonel William Moultrie, commander of the Second South Carolina Regiment. It is not known if this cloth was used to make the unit's colors, but in the colonel's memoirs he wrote: "it was thought necessary to have a flag for the purpose of signals: (as there was no national or state flag at the time) I was desired by the council of safety to have one made, upon which, as the state troops were clothed in blue, and the fort was garrisoned by the first and second regiments, who wore a silver crescent on the front of their cap; I had a large blue flag made with a crescent in the dexter corner, to be uniform with the troops: This was the first American flag which was displayed in South-Carolina."

Ordered to Sullivan's Island, the Second South Carolina was the principal command in the island's half-completed palmetto log and sand fort, and the regiment's colors served as the garrison's flag. During the June 28, 1776, attack by a British fleet, the flagstaff was cut down by artillery. Sergeant William Jasper retrieved the colors, tied them to a staff, and planted them back on the ramparts. The British were defeated, providing the patriot cause its first major victory in the Revolutionary War. In January 1861, after the state's secession from the Union, the legislature drew on the symbolism of the Second South Carolina's colors and the fort's palmetto logs to adopt the official flag of South Carolina. RICHARD W. HATCHER III

Moultrie, William. *Memoirs of the American Revolution.* 1802. Reprint, New York: New York Times, 1968.

Wates, Wylma A. *A Flag Worthy of Your State and People: The History of the South Carolina State Flag.* 2d ed. Columbia: South Carolina Department of Archives and History, 1990.

NINETY SIX, BATTLES OF (1775, 1781). Situated in the South Carolina backcountry at the crossroads of important trade routes, Ninety Six was a newly established courthouse town on the eve of the Revolutionary War. The question of independence deeply divided the inhabitants of the district. For many colonists, land grants and protection from Indian incursions created strong devotion toward Great Britain. Others thought that the crown had shirked promises of better government to backcountry settlers and favored independence. With mounting tensions and the absence of British authority, conflict began in the South Carolina backcountry as a civil war.

On July 12, 1775, patriot forces seized nearby Fort Charlotte on the Savannah River. Returning to Ninety Six with captured ammunition, the triumphant party was met by a group of Loyalists who had been informed by a defector from the patriot ranks. The affair ended without bloodshed, and the gunpowder was returned to the fort. Fighting was narrowly averted again a few weeks later when Tory forces gathered and threatened. Whig political leader William Henry Drayton and Major Andrew Williamson countered with a show of force, and the standoff ended with both sides agreeing to a truce on September 16. Weeks later a force of eighteen hundred Loyalists attacked one-third that number of patriots under Williamson, who gathered Whig forces in a hastily erected stockade near Ninety Six on November 18, 1775. The two groups had been jockeying for control of a supply of gunpowder and lead sent to the Cherokees by the colonial government. After three days of fighting with few casualties, the two sides agreed to a brief truce. Although neither side admitted defeat, Loyalist forces failed to recover the ammunition and withdrew. A month later, a substantial patriot force mounted an expedition, the so-called "Snow Campaign," to crush organized Loyalist opposition.

The following year saw an increase in attacks on settlements in Ninety Six District by hostile Cherokees. In late July 1776 Williamson, now a brigadier general, mounted a punitive expedition into the Cherokee Nation, which ended in October. The village of Ninety Six experienced a period of relative peace for the next few years. Although Loyalists remained in the region, the courthouse village retained Whig rule. Crown forces, however, shifted their strategic focus from the northern to the southern colonies with the capture of Savannah in December 1778. Charleston fell in May 1780. Lieutenant Colonel Nisbet Balfour was quickly dispatched up the Cherokee Path to deal with any patriot militia still under arms in the Upcountry. Arriving at Ninety Six in late June, he found that rebel leaders had surrendered the fort and munitions to royal authority a few days earlier. By the end of the year, the British had strengthened the old fort's defenses and established Ninety Six as a depot and meeting ground for Tories.

Losses at King's Mountain, Cowpens, and other engagements set the British on less than sure footing in South Carolina by February 1781. After the Battle of Guilford Court House in North Carolina in mid-March, the British commander in the South, Lord Cornwallis, retired to the North Carolina coast with his battered army. Instead of pursuing, the American commander, Major General Nathanael Greene, set out to reduce the chain of posts in occupied South Carolina. Royal forces soon surrendered or abandoned many positions in the northern and central parts of the state, and Greene turned his attention to the western garrison at Ninety Six. American forces arrived in late May. With his chief engineer, Colonel Thaddeus Kosciuszko, Greene surveyed the fortifications and decided to lay siege to the Star Fort, then under the command of New York Loyalist Colonel John Harris Cruger.

For twenty-eight days the small American army steadily dug siege lines and defended them against frequent sallies by the fort's defenders. Other means were tried as well. But on June 17 word of a British relief column reached the besieged village. Greene reluctantly ordered an assault the next day, and for nearly an hour his soldiers bravely tried to breach the fort's defenses without success. When Cruger's men counterattacked successfully, the American commander ordered a retreat. The American army withdrew from Ninety Six two days before British reinforcements arrived. Afterward British commanders deemed the post untenable and abandoned their position within the week. The departing British Army demolished the fortifications and set fire to the few buildings still standing. The civil war would linger in the region for many months, but the withdrawal marked the end of a British presence at Ninety Six. SAMUEL K. FORE

Bass, Robert D. *Ninety Six: The Struggle for the South Carolina Back Country.* Lexington, S.C.: Sandlapper Store, 1978.

Cann, Marvin L. "Prelude to War: The First Battle of Ninety-Six, November 19–21, 1775." *South Carolina Historical Magazine* 76 (October 1975): 197–214.

———. "War in the Backcountry: The Siege of Ninety Six, May 22–June 19, 1781." *South Carolina Historical Magazine* 72 (January 1971): 1–14.

Greene, Jerome A. *Ninety Six: A Historical Narrative.* Denver, Colo.: U.S. Department of the Interior, 1978.

PARKER'S FERRY, BATTLE OF (August 30, 1781). During the summer of 1781, Tories roved the countryside surrounding Charleston. Patriot colonel William Harden commanded a dwindling militia force south of the Edisto River and requested assistance from Brigadier General Francis Marion to counter this threat. Arriving at the village of Round "O" on August 22, Marion set out to gather intelligence. He learned that a force of one hundred Tories under Colonel William "Bloody Bill" Cunningham was assembling on the banks of the Pon Pon River (present-day Edisto River) to join a larger body of British and Hessian regulars and Loyalist militiamen. Marion quickly prepared an ambush to prevent the juncture.

On August 30 the patriot force took position in the thick woods of a swamp about forty yards from the road and within a mile of Parker's Ferry. A few light horsemen were sent forward as decoys. As the British force approached in the late afternoon, a Tory sentry noticed a white cockade—the mark of Marion's men—in a soldier's cap in the woodline. Musket fire was exchanged, and the horsemen charged, forcing the Tories back toward the ferry. From a distance, British lieutenant colonel DeBorck watched the engagement and ordered Major Thomas Fraser to charge with his dragoons. Fraser's men galloped blindly into the trap. As the British cavalrymen came abreast of the American position, they received several volleys of fire. Low on ammunition, Marion withdrew when a column of enemy infantrymen arrived on the scene. British losses were estimated at about twenty-five killed and eighty wounded, with minimal harm to Marion's force. This small but effective engagement checked the British cavalry and put a stop to the marauding of the Tories so that they never posed a threat in the region again. SAMUEL K. FORE

Daso, Dik A. "Colonel William Harden: The Unsung Partisan Commander." *Proceedings of the South Carolina Historical Association* (1995): 95–111.

James, William Dobein. *A Sketch of the Life of Brig. Gen. Francis Marion.* 1821. Reprint, Marietta, Ga.: Continental Book Company, 1948.

Lumpkin, Henry. *From Savannah to Yorktown: The American Revolution in the South.* Columbia: University of South Carolina Press, 1981.

PARTISANS. After the fall of Charleston in May 1780, bands of partisans, or irregular soldiers, sprang up to fight royal control of South Carolina during the Revolutionary War. Subsequently, many backcountry militiamen surrendered and were paroled to their homes instead of serving as prisoners of war. Some refused, however, and fled across the Savannah River to join rebel forces in Georgia. In the meantime, crown forces established garrisons in key parts in the interior of the state, all the while committing depredations against the conquered, including the massacre at the Waxhaws. Moreover, British commander Sir Henry Clinton revoked the paroles of rebel militiamen and required them to join Loyalist militias or be considered fugitives.

In an attempt to preserve state government, Governor John Rutledge fled Charleston in April, and he later moved into North Carolina as the British army advanced inland. With the perception of no real civil authority, many chose to oppose the British and Tories on their own "by force of arms," using organizations loosely based on the state's militia system. In the New Acquisition District (in the Catawba River Valley), patriots began almost immediately to organize and equip themselves for a campaign. In the first days of June 1780, Whig commanders John McClure and William Bratton struck successful blows against Tory forces gathering at Alexander's Old Field and Mobley's Meeting House.

Over the next few months partisan forces, under such commanders as Thomas Sumter and Francis Marion, began to make significant gains against occupying forces. These irregular forces sometimes met the enemy in open battle and other times made hit-and-run raids on vital supply and communication lines. By year's end, Lord Cornwallis, the British commander in the

South, was hindered in his intended advance into North Carolina. Practically all of Cornwallis's resources were engaged in pursuing partisan forces in portions of South Carolina. When General Nathanael Greene took command of the Continental army in late 1780, he wisely sought to incorporate partisan forces into his strategic plan for the following year. A prime example of this was his detaching Henry Lee's Legion to Brigadier General Francis Marion's command for the siege of Fort Motte in May 1781.

Several factors have been attributed to partisans' successes. Chief among them was their mobility as they were by and large inseparable from their horses. Although serious fighting was done dismounted, they were able to ride swiftly into and out of conflict and harass the enemy whenever and wherever possible. Some of them were trained, experienced soldiers, and the partisans were primarily residents of the South Carolina backcountry and were accustomed to hunting and defending themselves against Native Americans. Therefore, the frontiersmen were well trained with the weapons and tactics required for unconventional warfare. The partisans also had their particular problems. Oftentimes leaders, such as Sumter, refused to follow directives from General Greene. With little or no financial backing, partisans were plagued with reduced turnouts and desertions. Despite these difficulties, the partisans played a key role in derailing Clinton's southern strategy and in driving the British from South Carolina. SAMUEL K. FORE

Edgar, Walter. *Partisans and Redcoats: The Southern Conflict That Turned the Tide of the American Revolution.* New York: Morrow, 2001.

Ferguson, Clyde R. "Functions of the Partisan Militia in the South during the American Revolution: An Interpretation." In *The Revolutionary War in the South—Power, Conflict, and Leadership: Essays in Honor of John Richard Alden,* edited by W. Robert Higgins. Durham, N.C.: Duke University Press, 1979.

Weigley, Russell F. *The Partisan War: The South Carolina Campaign of 1780–1782.* Columbia: South Carolina Tricentennial Commission, 1970.

PICKENS, ANDREW (1739–1817). Soldier, legislator, congressman. Pickens was born in Paxtang Township, Pennsylvania, on September 19, 1739, the son of Andrew Pickens and Ann Davis. His family was among the Huguenots and Scots-Irish that settled in Northern Ireland and then migrated to Pennsylvania. After moving southward, the Pickens family eventually settled on Waxhaw Creek, South Carolina, by 1752. The young Pickens commenced his military service as a company grade officer in the Cherokee War of 1759–1761. After the hostilities, he moved to the Long Canes area of western South Carolina and married Rebecca Calhoun on March 19, 1765. The couple

Andrew Pickens. Courtesy, Library of Congress, Prints and Photographs Division.

had twelve children. This marriage formed ties with several prominent Up-country families.

During the Revolutionary War, Pickens became one of the most significant leaders of patriot forces in the South Carolina backcountry. He initially served as a militia company commander for Ninety Six District and campaigned against Tories in late 1775. By 1778 he had attained the rank of colonel of the Upper Ninety Six Regiment and had participated in expeditions against the British-allied Cherokees and the unsuccessful American invasion of East Florida. The most severe check of the Loyalists in the backcountry came on February 14, 1779, when patriots crushed the Loyalist force at Kettle Creek, Georgia. After the surrender of Charleston, Pickens took British protection and was paroled to his home. He renounced protection, however, when the British failed to prevent a Loyalist band from plundering his plantation. At the Battle of Cowpens on January 17, 1781, Pickens was in charge of the South Carolina militia during the decisive victory over Lieutenant Colonel Banastre Tarleton's British forces. Afterward, Pickens was named a brigadier general by Governor John Rutledge and cooperated with General Nathanael Greene's objective of isolating British posts in the South Carolina interior. Wounded at the Battle of Eutaw Springs in September 1781, Pickens recovered to wage two more punitive campaigns against the Cherokees in mid-1782.

After the war, Pickens served as both a legislator and a negotiator with the Native Americans. He represented Ninety Six District in the state House of Representatives from 1776 to 1788 and Pendleton District in the state Senate from 1790 to 1793. He resigned his Senate seat upon his election to the U.S. House of Representatives, where he served from 1793 to 1795. As a legislator, Pickens worked to establish schools, churches, and a legal system for the South Carolina backcountry. A recognized expert on Indian affairs, Pickens served as a federal commissioner to negotiate peace independently with the Cherokees, Chickasaws, Choctaws, and Creeks in the late 1780s and eventually negotiated a firm peace with the Treaty of Coleraine in 1796. The following year he and Benjamin Hawkins surveyed most of the southern boundary line between the United States and the Indian nations.

Pickens served two more terms in the General Assembly from 1796 to 1799, representing Pendleton District. He retired to his plantation Tamassee in 1805, coming out only briefly in 1812 when elected to a final term in the General Assembly to prepare South Carolina for war. He died at Tamassee on August 11, 1817, and was buried at the Old Stone Presbyterian Church. SAMUEL K. FORE

Ferguson, Clyde R. "General Andrew Pickens." Ph.D. diss., Duke University, 1960.

Skelton, Lynda Worley, ed. *General Andrew Pickens: An Autobiography.* Pendleton, S.C.: Pendleton District Historical and Recreational Commission, 1976.

Waring, Alice Noble. *The Fighting Elder: Andrew Pickens (1739–1817).* Columbia: University of South Carolina Press, 1962.

PINCKNEY, CHARLES

PINCKNEY, CHARLES (1757–1824). Planter, legislator, governor, statesman. Pinckney was born in Charleston on October 26, 1757, the son of Charles Pinckney and Frances Brewton. Little is known of his childhood. In 1773, while still in his teens, he enrolled in the Middle Temple in London, but the Revolution prevented him from attending. As a result, he received most of his education in Charleston, first under the tutelage of Dr. David Oliphant and later in the law office of his father.

In 1779 Pinckney entered public service as a representative to the General Assembly from Christ Church Parish, home of his family's country estate, Snee Farm. During the Revolution he joined the Charleston militia and saw action at the siege of Savannah (September–October 1779) and was captured at the fall of Charleston in May 1780. After being confined on board the prison ship *Pack Horse,* Pinckney was eventually paroled in a general prisoner exchange in the summer of 1781. Following his release, he went to Philadelphia. After his father died in September 1782, Pinckney returned to

Charles Pinckney. Courtesy, New York Public Library.

South Carolina the following year to assist his mother in settling the estate and to resume his political career. In 1784 Pinckney reentered the General Assembly and, later that year, was elected to the Confederation Congress.

In Congress, Pinckney quickly made a name for himself. He became friends with James Monroe and served with the Virginian on a committee responsible for presenting Thomas Jefferson's ordinances regarding the Northwest Territory. Pinckney also spoke forcefully regarding negotiations with Spain, stressing that securing navigation rights to the Mississippi River for the United States was imperative to southern interests. In 1786 Pinckney was one of three members appointed to persuade the New Jersey assembly to pay their share of Confederation taxes. In his address, Pinckney suggested that if they did not agree with the operation of the government, they should call a convention to try to make necessary improvements. Making a similar call two months later in the Confederation Congress, Pinckney submitted a plan for amending the Articles of Confederation to give more power to the national government, especially in the regulation of commerce. His plan was put aside, however, when word came from Annapolis that a call had been made for a convention of the states to reconsider the powers of the federal government. Because of his outspoken belief that the Articles of Confederation were defective and his eloquence regarding the subject, the South Carolina General Assembly elected Pinckney as one of the five South Carolinians to attend the May 1787 constitutional convention in Philadelphia, where he became one of the convention's most active delegates.

On the third day of the convention he submitted what came to be known as "The Pinckney Draft," which was similar to the "Virginia Plan" of Edmund Randolph. Pinckney's proposal called for a strong central government consisting of three "separate and distinct" branches. The legislative branch would consist of a Senate and a House of Delegates. The House would be elected proportionately to the white population, with slaves being counted as three-fifths of a person toward representation. To fill the Senate, the states would be divided into districts according to size. The larger the size of the state, the more senators it would have. The legislature would be responsible for national defense, "regulating the Trade with the several States as well with Foreign Nations as with each other," forming a post office, regulating Indian affairs, coining money, "ordering the Militia of any State to any Place within the U.S.," choosing the president, and "instituting a federal judicial Court." The president would serve for a term of seven years and be responsible for informing the legislature "at every session of the condition of the United States." In other words, the president would deliver what have come to be known as "State of the Union Addresses." The president would also be the commander in chief of the military and would inspect the various departments within the government. He would have the power to call members of the legislature into emergency session and to dismiss them "when they cannot agree as to the time of their adjournment." The House of Delegates would have power of impeachment, with senators and federal judges holding the power to try the executive. The judicial branch, appointed by the legislature, would hear cases brought against United States officers and settle matters between states and between a state and the federal government. There would also be a court of admiralty. Judges would be appointed for a term of "good Behavior," although the manner of appointment was not specified. Pinckney even attached a small "Bill of Rights" to his document, which provided for "the privilege of the writ of habeas corpus—the trial by jury in all cases, criminal as well as civil—the freedom of the press and the prevention of religious tests as qualifications to offices of trust or emolument." Although his plan was not adopted in its entirety, dozens of Pinckney's proposals found their way into what would become the United States Constitution.

One of the most important moments for Pinckney during the convention came on June 25. Speaking to his fellow delegates, he made a forceful case for the unique quality of America and the importance of seeking original solutions for a new government. The address was redolent with republican ideology, such as calling for a nation led by an aristocracy based on merit, not birth, as well as themes that influenced Jacksonian democracy in the next century.

After the convention, Pinckney returned to South Carolina and married Mary Eleanor Laurens, daughter of Henry Laurens, on April 27, 1788. The following month he served at the state ratifying convention, speaking in support of the new constitution he had helped to create and reiterating the themes of his June 25, 1787, speech in Philadelphia. In doing so, he sought to placate backcountry delegates, who feared that the document would benefit the state's Lowcountry elite and the northern states at the expense of their liberty. Supporters of the document, however, outweighed the opposition, and South Carolina ratified the Constitution by a vote of 149 to 73.

Pinckney was elected governor in 1789 and became the first to serve at the new capital of Columbia, basing his political operations from his plantation Greenwich, on the Congaree River just south of town. He also presided over the state constitutional convention of 1790. Using his considerable political influence, he organized backcountry dissidents into a voting bloc that, ten years later, would back his support of Thomas Jefferson's bid for the presidency. In supporting Jefferson, Pinckney broke with his economic base, his geographic roots in the Lowcountry, and his family (his cousin Charles Cotesworth Pinckney was Jefferson's opponent) in order to unite the state and insure the election of his ideological peer.

When U.S. Senator John Hunter resigned from Congress in November 1798, Pinckney was appointed to serve out his term. However, after Jefferson's election as president in 1800, Pinckney was named minister plenipotentiary to Spain. From 1801 to 1805 he attempted to conduct foreign affairs but found himself hampered by an arrogant Spanish court and a secretary of state, James Madison, who believed Pinckney to be inept in diplomatic matters. Returning to South Carolina in 1806, Pinckney was reelected governor in December and served a record fourth term. Although he may have alienated his family and his socioeconomic peers, as well as some in his own party, the majority of the people in South Carolina respected his ability and his willingness to reach across class and geographic lines in order to unite the state. He served in various state offices until 1814, when he retired from public life. The respite was brief, however, and in 1819 Pinckney was elected to the U.S. House of Representatives. There he spoke in opposition to the Missouri Compromise, claiming that it threatened southern interests, particularly slavery, and paving the way for later southern advocates such as

John C. Calhoun. Declining reelection in 1821, Pinckney left the public arena for good.

On October 29, 1824, Pinckney died in Charleston, and he was buried in the graveyard at St. Philip's Church. He was survived by a daughter, Mary Eleanor Pinckney, and a son, Henry Laurens Pinckney, whose birth had claimed the life of his mother in 1794. Another daughter, Frances Henrietta Pinckney, had predeceased her father. Scorned by his class and his family for much of his latter life, Pinckney was also dismissed by some historians as vain, arrogant, and too willing to take credit for the work of others. He was actually an important transitional figure at both the state and national levels. He succeeded in uniting his state across class and geographic lines to insure Jefferson's election in 1800 and, in doing so, earned distinction as a founder of the Democratic Party in South Carolina. On a national level, he bridged the generation gap between the founding fathers of the revolutionary period and their successors in the age of Andrew Jackson. MARTY D. MATTHEWS

Kaplanoff, Mark D. "Charles Pinckney and the American Republican Tradition." In *Intellectual Life in Antebellum Charleston,* edited by Michael O'Brien and David Moltke-Hansen. Knoxville: University of Tennessee Press, 1986.

Matthews, Marty D. *Forgotten Founder: The Life and Times of Charles Pinckney.* Columbia: University of South Carolina Press, 2004.

Williams, Frances Leigh. *A Founding Family: The Pinckneys of South Carolina.* New York: Harcourt Brace Jovanovich, 1978.

PINCKNEY, CHARLES COTESWORTH (1746–1825). Soldier, statesman, diplomat. Pinckney was born in Charleston on February 14, 1746, to Charles Pinckney, a lawyer and member of the provincial council, and Elizabeth Lucas, who helped introduce indigo cultivation in South Carolina. In 1753 Pinckney accompanied his family to London, where his father served as the colony's agent until 1758. Young Pinckney received private tutoring before entering the prestigious Westminster School in 1761. Three years later he matriculated at both Christ Church College, Oxford, and at the Middle Temple, the London legal training ground. While at Oxford he attended lectures by the famed legal scholar Sir William Blackstone and listened to debates in the House of Commons pertaining to the American colonies. Pinckney was admitted to the English Bar in January 1769. Following a tour of Europe, he returned to South Carolina, where he began a successful legal practice.

Pinckney entered public service in 1769 with election to the Commons House of Assembly, where he represented St. John's Colleton Parish during the remainder of royal rule. Pinckney also served in the local militia, eventually attaining the rank of colonel. In 1773 he was made attorney general for the judicial districts of Camden, Cheraws, and Georgetown. That same year, on September 28, he married Sarah Middleton, daughter of the wealthy and well-connected Henry Middleton. The marriage produced four children. Through this marriage Pinckney became closely affiliated with some of the province's leading radicals in America's contest with Great Britain, such as Arthur Middleton, Edward Rutledge, and William Henry Drayton. By early 1775 Pinckney was a member of all the important revolutionary committees, from which he advocated aggressive measures, including stealing royal arms from the State House, penning inflammatory epistles to backcountry inhabitants, and planning the defense of Charleston against a possible British attack. At the same time, Pinckney served in the extralegal Provincial Congress, where he assisted in creating and training a rebel army and chaired the committee responsible for drafting a temporary frame of government for the province.

Once hostilities erupted with Britain, Pinckney switched his role as a politician to that of a soldier. Appointed commander of the First Regiment of South Carolina troops, he assisted in the successful defense of Charleston at the Battle of Sullivan's Island in June 1776. When the British moved north following this defeat, Pinckney followed to serve as an aide-de-camp to General George Washington. He participated at the battles of Brandywine and Germantown before rejoining the southern army to command a regiment in the expedition to East Florida and at the siege of Savannah. During the defense of Charleston he commanded Fort Moultrie and made a futile attempt to convince General Benjamin Lincoln, commander of the southern army, to defend the capital at all costs. When Charleston fell, the British placed Pinckney under house arrest and made a hapless attempt to lure him away from the American cause. The British later sent Pinckney to Philadelphia, where he was exchanged in 1782. He rejoined the southern army but saw no further action. Pinckney's first wife, Sarah Middleton, died in 1784, and he married Mary Stead in 1786.

Following the war, Pinckney devoted his efforts toward rebuilding his law practice and his rice plantations. In 1787 he served as a delegate to the constitutional convention, where he ardently and ably defended the exporting and slaveholding interests of southern planters. A staunch Federalist, Pinckney was important in South Carolina's ratification of the federal Constitution in 1788. He later helped draft the state's 1790 constitution. Over the next several years Pinckney rejected President Washington's numerous offers to serve in federal office—as commander of the army, as associate

Charles Cotesworth Pinckney. Oil on canvas, ca. 1773. Courtesy, National Portrait Gallery, Smithsonian Institution.

justice of the Supreme Court, as secretary of war, and as secretary of state—explaining that he needed to remain at home to restore his fortune. However, in 1796 Pinckney accepted Washington's offer to serve as minister to France. The next year President John Adams appointed him as one of three commissioners to negotiate a treaty with the French government. When French diplomats demanded a bribe from their American counterparts to facilitate discussions, Pinckney is credited as having exclaimed "no! no! Not a sixpense" and urged his government to raise "millions for defence but not one cent for tribute." In 1798 President Adams, anticipating war with France, appointed Pinckney commander of the southern department of the United States Army. He was discharged from military service in 1800.

Pinckney returned to politics in the election of 1800 as the Federalist Party's vice-presidential candidate. In 1804 and 1808 he was the Federalist candidate for president, but realizing that he had little chance of winning, he never actively campaigned. Instead, Pinckney devoted the remainder of his life to agricultural experiments (he was a member of the South Carolina Agricultural Society) and civic service. He helped establish South Carolina College in 1801 and served on its first board of trustees. He also busied himself as president of numerous organizations, including the South Carolina Jockey Club, the Society for the Relief of Widows and Orphans of South Carolina, the Charleston Bible Society, the Charleston Library Society, the South Carolina Society of the Cincinnati, and the national Society of the

Cincinnati. Near the end of his life Pinckney campaigned against dueling in South Carolina. He died in Charleston on August 16, 1825 and was buried in the cemetery of St. Michael's Church. KEITH KRAWCZYNSKI

Rogers, George C. *Charleston in the Age of the Pinckneys.* Rev. ed. Columbia: University of South Carolina Press, 1980.

Williams, Francis Leigh. *A Founding Family: The Pinckneys of South Carolina.* New York: Harcourt Brace Jovanovich, 1978.

Zahniser, Marvin R. *Charles Cotesworth Pinckney: Founding Father.* Chapel Hill: University of North Carolina Press, 1967.

PINCKNEY, THOMAS (1750–1828). Governor, diplomat, congressman, soldier. Pinckney was born in Charleston on October 23, 1750, the son of Charles Pinckney and Elizabeth "Eliza" Lucas, and the brother of Charles Cotesworth Pinckney. In 1753 the Pinckneys sailed to England to educate their sons. When their parents returned to South Carolina in 1758, the boys remained behind. Thomas Pinckney received a liberal education at Westminster School and Christ College, Oxford, and studied law at the Middle Temple in the Inns of Court. In addition, he briefly attended the Royal Military Academy in Caen, France, where he studied military science. After his return to Charleston in December 1774, he was admitted to the South Carolina Bar and commenced his law practice.

At the outbreak of war in 1775, Pinckney became a captain in the First South Carolina Continental regiment and was later promoted to major. He traveled to North Carolina and Virginia on recruiting missions and supervised the construction of fortifications. Much of his early service involved tedious garrison duty in Charleston harbor. At one point he wryly reassured his sister Harriott that she need not worry "for you may depend upon their being no fighting wherever I am." Pinckney subsequently participated in the failed invasion of East Florida in 1778. When the British invaded South Carolina in May 1779, they burned Pinckney's Aukland Plantation on the Ashepoo River. That fall Pinckney served as a liaison between American and French forces at the siege of Savannah. During a lull in the fighting, he married Elizabeth Motte on July 22, 1779. Their union produced six children. Three years after Elizabeth's death, he married her sister, Frances, on October 19, 1797. Pinckney's second marriage produced two children.

When the British laid siege to Charleston in 1780, Pinckney urged that the city be defended. Because General Benjamin Lincoln sent him to search for expected reinforcements, he avoided capture when the city surrendered in May. He then joined the remaining Continental troops in the Carolinas

Thomas Pinckney. Oil on wood panel, 1791. Courtesy, National Portrait Gallery, Smithsonian Institution.

and became General Horatio Gates's aide-de-camp. At the Battle of Camden on August 16, 1780, Pinckney's leg was shattered by a musket ball and he was captured, ending his active service in the war. The British paroled him, and he spent time in Philadelphia and Virginia before returning to South Carolina. After the war, he publicly defended Gates's strategic and tactical decisions.

Pinckney shifted his attention from practicing law to planting and politics. He represented the city parishes of St. Philip's and St. Michael's in the state House of Representatives from 1776 until 1791. He was elected governor of South Carolina on February 20, 1787, and served two years. He submitted the federal Constitution to the state legislature and presided over the ratification convention that met in Charleston in 1788. Three years after leaving office in 1789, Pinckney accepted the prestigious and challenging appointment as U.S. minister to Great Britain on January 16, 1792.

As a diplomat, Pinckney was competent rather than brilliant. To his frustration, he was unable to secure compensation for slaves removed by the British or resolve disputes over British fortifications in the Northwest and American fishing rights off Newfoundland. When Britain and France went to war in 1793, the United States found its neutrality threatened. Hoping to avert war, President George Washington sent John Jay in 1794 on a special mission to Britain. Despite his disappointment at being temporarily superseded, Pinckney charitably supported the mission and approved the controversial treaty that Jay negotiated.

Pinckney's moment did come, however, for in November 1794 he was appointed envoy extraordinary to Spain. From June to October 1795 Pinckney worked to settle territorial and commercial disputes between the United States and Spain. He considered indispensable the American right to deposit and ship goods from the mouth of the Mississippi River. To secure this point and end the diplomatic stalemate, he demanded his passport, which caused his counterpart, Manuel de Godoy, the prince of peace, to concede. The Treaty of San Lorenzo, signed on October 27, 1795, granted Americans the privilege (rather than the right) to use the port of New Orleans and established a clear boundary between the United States and West Florida. Pinckney's mission to Spain proved to be the high point of a long public career. The treaty he negotiated paved the way for American settlement of the Southeast and for future territorial acquisitions from the French and the Spanish.

In 1796 Pinckney resigned his European post and returned to South Carolina. Before he arrived, the Federalists nominated him as their candidate for vice president. Because of political maneuvering, Pinckney finished behind Thomas Jefferson in the voting. In November 1797 Pinckney was elected to the U.S. House of Representatives to complete William Smith's unexpired term. In Congress he generally supported the Adams administration's preparations for war with France, but he opposed the Sedition Act. He left Congress in 1801 and, except for another term in the General Assembly from 1802 to 1804, withdrew from public life.

His retirement ended during the War of 1812, when he was commissioned a major general and given command of the Southern Division of the U.S. Army. He worked to strengthen coastal fortifications and held overall command during the war with the Creeks, but he saw no action. After the war, Pinckney retired to his plantation on the Santee River, which he named El Dorado. Noted for his agricultural innovations, which included using dikes to reclaim saltwater marshes for rice cultivation and importing choice cattle from Europe, he contributed articles to the *Southern Agriculturist* and reports to the Agricultural Society. In 1825 he became president general of the national Society of the Cincinnati. On November 2, 1828, Pinckney died in Charleston. He was buried in St. Philip's Churchyard. GREGORY D. MASSEY

Bemis, Samuel Flagg. "The London Mission of Thomas Pinckney, 1792–1796." *American Historical Review* 27 (January 1923): 228–47.

———. *Pinckney's Treaty: America's Advantage from Europe's Distress, 1783–1800*. Rev. ed. New Haven, Conn.: Yale University Press, 1960.

Pinckney, Charles Cotesworth. *Life of General Thomas Pinckney*. Boston: Houghton, Mifflin, 1895.

Williams, Frances Leigh. *A Founding Family: The Pinckneys of South Carolina*. New York: Harcourt Brace Jovanovich, 1978.

PORT ROYAL ISLAND, BATTLE OF (February 3, 1779). The Battle of Port Royal Island was part of a larger campaign designed by the British to cover their operations against Augusta, Georgia. On February 2, 1779, while British units were marching on Augusta from Savannah, an amphibious expedition consisting of 150 light infantrymen on four transports, the twenty-four-gun ship *Vigilant,* and the smaller warship *Germaine* left Tybee Island, Georgia, for Port Royal. The approach of the British warships forced the patriots to destroy Fort Lyttleton at Beaufort. But instead of occupying Beaufort, the British continued into the Broad River and destroyed the homes of Stephen Bull and Thomas Heyward, Sr.

The next day, February 3, the British continued up the Broad River and landed the light infantrymen under Major William Gardner on Port Royal Island. The soldiers marched to Port Royal Ferry but found it well protected. While returning to their transports, the British discovered a force of four hundred militiamen and some Continental artillerymen under Generals Stephen Bull and William Moultrie drawn up across the road on a rise known as Grey's Hill. Though outnumbered, the British attacked. In a sharp fight lasting forty-five minutes, the Americans suffered about thirty casualties, while the British lost about seventy-five men. At the end of the battle both sides withdrew. The British remained in the area and gathered up slaves and were joined by Loyalists before returning to Savannah. Though the campaign was inconclusive, it did demonstrate the ability of the British to use their command of the waterways to strike at both military and civilian targets and to strengthen the resolve of South Carolina Loyalists. STEPHEN R. WISE

Butler, Lewis W. G. *Annals of the King's Rifle Corps*. Vol. 1. London: J. Murray, 1913.

Ripley, Warren. *Battleground: South Carolina in the Revolution*. Charleston, S.C.: Post-Courier, 1983.

Rowland, Lawrence S., Alexander Moore, and George C. Rogers. *The History of Beaufort County, South Carolina*. Vol. 1, *1514–1861*. Columbia: University of South Carolina Press, 1996.

Ward, Christopher. *The War of the Revolution*. 2 vols. New York: Macmillan, 1952.

PROVINCIALS. With tensions between Great Britain and her North American colonists coming to a boil, the crown found itself mobilizing for war in 1775. In addition to regular British soldiers and German mercenaries, British officials organized loyal Americans into conventional fighting units commonly referred to as provincials. A provincial soldier was a volunteer subject to the same control, benefits, and hardships as a British soldier but was ineligible for allowances and perquisites equal to those received by regular troops.

In South Carolina, Loyalists stepped forward in reaction to the actions of the Committee of Safety during the summer of 1775. However, British field commanders and civil administrators, expecting the war to be over quickly, did not raise many provincial units. By 1778 events in the northern theater caused the British high command to reexamine its strategy and turn its attention southward.

Emboldened by successes in Georgia in 1778 and 1779, the British army launched a major offensive against the patriot stronghold of Charleston, which surrendered on May 12, 1780. The South Carolina Royalists (a unit actually formed in East Florida from loyal refugees who were chiefly from Ninety Six District), the King's American Regiment, and the British Legion were provincial units instrumental in the royal victory. Moving into the backcountry, Lord Cornwallis actively sought to recruit provincial units in South Carolina. One such regiment, raised by John Harrison of the Pee Dee region, became known as the South Carolina Rangers.

Beset by decentralized leadership, unreliable support, and the determination of the patriots, provincials were not utilized to their full potential in the conflict. With the end of hostilities, the officers and men of the various provincial units chose to relocate to Canada, Britain, and the West Indies. SAMUEL K. FORE

Allen, Robert S., ed. *The Loyal Americans: The Military Role of the Loyalist Provincial Corps and Their Settlement in British North America, 1775–1784.* Ottawa, Canada: National Museums of Canada, 1983.

Bass, Robert D. "A Forgotten Loyalist Regiment: The South Carolina Rangers." *Proceedings of the South Carolina Historical Association* (1977): 64–71.

Lambert, Robert Stansbury. *South Carolina Loyalists in the American Revolution.* Columbia: University of South Carolina Press, 1987.

Shy, John. "British Strategy for Pacifying the Southern Colonies, 1778–1781." In *The Southern Experience in the American Revolution,* edited by Jeffery J. Crow and Larry E. Tise. Chapel Hill: University of North Carolina Press, 1978.

RAMSAY, DAVID (1749–1815). Physician, legislator, historian. Ramsay was born on April 2, 1749, in Lancaster County, Pennsylvania, the son of the Irish immigrant James Ramsay, a farmer, and Jane Montgomery. Intellectually precocious, Ramsay learned to read at an early age. As a youth, he tutored boys much older than himself. He graduated from the College of New Jersey (Princeton) in 1765 and received a bachelor of physic degree from the College of Philadelphia in 1773. He was later awarded an honorary doctor of medicine degree from Yale in 1803. After a brief practice in Maryland, Ramsay moved to Charleston in 1773 on the recommendation of his close friend and confidant Dr. Benjamin Rush. A Presbyterian, Ramsay quickly associated himself with the Independent Congregational Church in Charleston.

Ramsay's rise to position and influence in Charleston was rapid, and it was soon apparent that his activities would not be confined to medicine. He was an ardent supporter of the American Revolution and delivered a stirring speech in support of the American cause on July 4, 1778, at an anniversary celebration of the Declaration of Independence. Ramsay served as a military surgeon early in the war and was imprisoned in St. Augustine, Florida, by the British for eleven months with other patriots after the fall of Charleston in May 1780.

First elected to the South Carolina legislature by St. Philip's and St. Michael's Parishes in 1776, Ramsay was active in colonial and state politics during and after the war, eventually serving a total of twenty-three years in the South Carolina legislature, including six years as president of the Senate from 1791 to 1797. He was elected to the Confederation Congress in 1782 and served until 1786, serving as president pro tempore during his final term. He strongly supported the ratification of the U.S. Constitution and was morally opposed to slavery, but he saw no practical solution in the political, economic, and social climate of the times. His liberal views on slavery and his well-known friendship with northern abolitionists such as Benjamin Rush contributed to his failed bids for election to the U.S. House of Representatives in 1788 and the U.S. Senate in 1794.

In 1789 Ramsay was among the founders of the Medical Society of South Carolina, and he was elected its president in 1797. He was one of the first advocates of formal medical education in South Carolina, which came to fruition with the first graduating class of the Medical College of South Carolina ten years after his death. He was also the originator of many innovative measures for the improvement of the public health, including the successful introduction of a smallpox vaccination in South Carolina.

Ramsay's most lasting legacy, however, was as a historian, in which role he gained national and international renown. He produced six major works of history, including *History of the American Revolution* (1789), which went through six American editions by 1865 and was also published in English, French, Irish, German, and Dutch editions. Ramsay's *History* is recognized as a pioneering scholarly treatise on the war and has secured his place as one of the originators of the American historical consciousness. His other significant works include *History of the Revolution of South Carolina* (2 vols., 1785), *Review of the Improvements, Progress and the State of Medicine in the XVIIITH Century* (1801), *Life of George Washington* (1807), *History of South Carolina from Its First Settlement in 1670 to 1808* (2 vols., 1809), and a posthumously published three-volume *History of the United States* (1816–1817) and a twelve-volume *Universal History Americanized* (1819).

Ramsay's successes as a physician, legislator, and historian contrasted sharply with his lack of financial success. He was a visionary with little aptitude for business, and his investments almost never produced the expected return. He nevertheless figured prominently in such commercial and financial institutions as the Santee Canal, the Reciprocal Insurance Company, the Bank of the United States, the Catawba Company, the South Carolina Homespun Company, and the Hamilton Steamship Company.

Ramsay was married and widowed three times. He married Sabina Ellis on February 9, 1775. After her death in 1776, Ramsay on March 18, 1783, married Frances Witherspoon, the daughter of John Witherspoon, a signer of the Declaration of Independence and president of the College of New Jersey. She died in 1784 after giving birth to a son. His third marriage, on January 28, 1787, was to Martha Laurens, daughter of Henry Laurens. The couple had eleven children, eight of whom survived infancy, before Martha's death in 1811. Ramsay died on May 8, 1815, from gunshot wounds inflicted by a deranged patient. He was buried in the Circular Congregational Churchyard in Charleston. W. CURTIS WORTHINGTON

Shaffer, Arthur H. *To Be an American: David Ramsay and the Making of the American Consciousness.* Columbia: University of South Carolina Press, 1991.
Waring, Joseph I. *A History of Medicine in South Carolina.* Vol. 1, 1670–1825. Columbia: South Carolina Medical Association, 1964.

READ, JACOB (ca. 1752–1816). Lawyer, U.S. senator. Born around 1752 in Christ Church Parish, Read was the eldest son of the Charleston merchant James Read and Rebecca Bond. About 1759 Read's parents settled in Savannah, where he received his early education at a local boarding school. He began the study of law in 1768, and although admitted to the South Carolina Bar in 1773, he went on to Gray's Inn in London to further his legal studies. While there, Read joined other Americans in the British capital in petitioning against the Coercive Acts of 1774. Upon his return to South Carolina two years later, he assumed a captaincy in the Charleston militia. After the fall of the city in 1780, Read was one of sixty-five South Carolina patriots exiled by the British to St. Augustine, Florida. There, he landed in solitary confinement for twelve days as a result of "some imprudent expressions" in his correspondence. Refusing to admit any wrongdoing, he remained a prisoner in St. Mark's Castle for five months, until his exchange in July 1781.

With the restoration of civil government in South Carolina, Read in January 1782 took a seat in the Jacksonborough Assembly, where he represented the city parishes of St. Philip's and St. Michael's. He remained a member of the House of Representatives until 1794. During his first term, he served on the committee for the amercement of Loyalists and helped lead the opposition to the arming of blacks. The following year, on February 12, 1783, the General Assembly elected him to Congress. A delegate for two years, Read played an active part in deliberations that culminated in the Northwest Ordinance of 1787. He also lobbied to have the federal capital placed in a southerly location. Toward the end of his congressional tenure, on October 13, 1785, Read married Catherine Van Horne, daughter of the wealthy New York merchant David Van Horne. The couple had four children.

Read's time in Congress led him to chafe at the impotence of the federal government under the Articles of Confederation. "To be respected [Congress] must be enabled to enforce an Obedience to their Ordinance. . . . If this is denied Congress is I think an Unnecessary & Useless Burden." In the January 1788 debates on the Constitution in the state House of Representatives, Read spoke strongly in favor of the new plan of government. Representing Christ Church Parish at the state ratification convention the following May, Read also voted for it.

Chosen Speaker of the South Carolina House of Representatives in 1789, Read repeatedly offered himself for higher office without success. Finally, in 1794, he won election to the U.S. Senate, where he sat from 1795 to 1801. A Federalist with close ties to the mercantile community, Read cast the crucial vote necessary for ratification of the Jay Treaty, for which a Charleston mob opposing the accord hung him in effigy and threatened his home. Despite having been treated "exceedingly Cruelly" by John Rutledge in the wrangle over the treaty, Read struggled to get his fellow South Carolinian confirmed as chief justice of the United States Supreme Court, although he was unsuccessful. Through patronage, Read gained influence over local customs and excise services and the Charleston branch of the Bank of the United States, agencies of particular importance to his merchant allies. At the peak of his public career in the late 1790s, Read, with James Simons, headed the most powerful faction in state politics. In 1800, however, he narrowly lost a reelection bid to John Ewing Colhoun, with Read apparently "sacrificed" for his support of the administration of John Adams. Appointed a federal district judge by Adams under the Judiciary Act of 1801, Read never served, as the authorizing legislation was repealed before he could take office.

As a lawyer, Read achieved distinction at both the state and the federal bars. From 1776 to 1779 he acted as counsel for South Carolina. In 1786 he joined the defense in the sensational trial of William Clay Snipes for the dueling murder of Maurice Simons. In the mid-1790s he litigated a series of sensitive cases for the British vice consuls in Charleston and Savannah, who sought to use American courts to recover British vessels captured by French privateers. Despite his experiences during the Revolution, Read often represented British interests, which likely cemented his reputation for being "decidedly anti-Gallican." In 1795 Read became the first South Carolinian to argue before the U.S. Supreme Court.

Although given to "wonderful pomposity," Read was deemed "a sensible, as well as a very good-natured man." He died in Charleston on July 17, 1816, survived by his wife and children. ROBERT F. KARACHUK

Bailey, N. Louise, and Elizabeth Ivey Cooper, eds. *Biographical Directory of the South Carolina House of Representatives.* Vol. 3, *1775–1790.* Columbia: University of South Carolina Press, 1981.

REVOLUTIONARY CONSTITUTIONS. South Carolina has adopted seven constitutions during the state's history, the first three of which were adopted in the eighteenth century. The first of these state constitutions was written in 1776 with subsequent documents adopted in 1778 and 1790. All of these documents were legislative enactments, and none were presented to the people for ratification. South Carolina would not have a popularly ratified constitution until 1868.

South Carolina became a free and independent state on March 26, 1776, more than three months before the Declaration of Independence. The state's Provincial Congress adopted a temporary plan of government that was to last until the disputes with Great Britain could be settled. The Provincial Congress dissolved into the S.C. General Assembly with a popularly elected lower house, which then elected thirteen of its members to an upper house.

It also elected a chief executive, or "president," a vice president, and a chief justice. John Rutledge was elected as the first president and Henry Laurens as the first vice president. Under the 1776 constitution, political power stayed firmly in legislative hands and with Lowcountry legislators. The Upcountry area had a large White population but was permitted to elect only 64 of the 202 members of the General Assembly.

Under the 1778 constitution, "president" was replaced by "governor," who was still elected by the General Assembly. Executive power, which had been substantial under the 1776 Constitution and included an absolute veto authority, was greatly reduced. The Anglican Church was disestablished, and the upper house became the popularly elected S.C. Senate. The representation imbalance in the legislature was adjusted so that the Upcountry share approached 41 percent. In 1786 the General Assembly relocated the capital from Charleston to Columbia, symbolizing increased statewide unity. The following year the General Assembly banned the importation of new enslaved persons. On May 23, 1788, South Carolina ratified the U.S. Constitution.

With the ratification of the new federal constitution came a need for a new state constitution, and South Carolina set about drafting its third constitution in less than fifteen years. Lowcountry parishes received the majority of delegates to the convention, and the constitution that they drafted made few concessions to the Upcountry. The state was divided into twenty-two counties, each with a court, but Lowcountry parishes continued as election districts for the House of Representatives. The total number of House members was reduced from 208 to 124, and the Upcountry did receive a small boost in representation. Of significance, though, efforts to have proportional representation in the House and to mandate regular reapportionment, both of which would have increased the power of the Upcountry, were both defeated easily. It was not until the constitution was amended in 1808 that proportional representation—set at one representative for each 1/62 of White population and one representative for every 1/62 of taxes collected—was realized. COLE BLEASE GRAHAM, JR.

Edgar, Walter. *South Carolina, A History*. Columbia: University of South Carolina Press, 1998.

Green, Fletcher M. *Constitutional Development in the South Atlantic States, 1776–1860: A Study in the Evolution of Democracy*. 1930. Reprint, New York: Da Capo, 1971.

Tarr, G. Alan. *Understanding State Constitutions*. Princeton, N.J.: Princeton University Press, 1998.

Underwood, James L. *The Constitution of South Carolina*. 4 vols. Columbia: University of South Carolina Press, 1986–1994.

RICHARDSON, DORCAS NELSON (ca. 1741–1834). Revolutionary War heroine. Richardson was the daughter of Jared Nelson (Neilson), who operated Nelson's Ferry on the Santee River in what later became Sumter District. In 1761 she married Richard Richardson, Jr. (1741–ca. 1816), son of Richard Richardson and Mary Cantey. The couple had ten children.

Dorcas Richardson's husband was the captain of a militia company and was taken prisoner after the surrender of Charleston. The British held him at Johns Island, where he became ill with smallpox. After recovering, he escaped and hid out in the swamps of the Santee River near his home. Meanwhile, British colonel Banastre Tarleton had made the Richardson house a cavalry station. Richardson's family was confined to a few rooms of their house and received little to eat. Nevertheless, Dorcas Richardson managed to send food and even a horse into the swamp for her husband while the British troops hunted for him. The British allegedly taunted Richardson with what they would do to her husband when they captured him.

After her husband succeeded in joining Francis Marion's troops, the British changed their tactics on Richardson. Using flattery and promises of wealth and promotion, they tried to persuade Dorcas to convince her husband to change to the British side. She defiantly refused their advances, however, "and refused to be made instrumental to their purposes." While the reports of British cruelty to Dorcas Richardson may have been exaggerated, they and other similar stories became anti-British propaganda to rally South Carolinians to the patriot cause. Richardson died in 1834. BRENDA THOMPSON SCHOOLFIELD

Bailey, N. Louise, and Elizabeth Ivey Cooper, eds. *Biographical Directory of the South Carolina House of Representatives.* Vol. 3, *1775–1790.* Columbia: University of South Carolina Press, 1981.

Ellet, Elizabeth F. *The Women of the American Revolution.* 2 vols. New York: Baker and Scribner, 1848.

RICHARDSON, RICHARD (ca. 1705–1780). Legislator, soldier. Richardson was born in Virginia and immigrated to South Carolina in the 1730s, settling on the upper Santee River in Prince Frederick's Parish. Through grants he amassed substantial landholdings and became a prosperous planter. On October 11, 1738, he married Mary Cantey. The couple had seven children. Mary died in 1767, and Richardson then married Dorothy Sinkler. His second marriage produced four sons. Richardson would be the founder of one of South Carolina's leading political families, with six of his descendants becoming governor of the state.

In the 1750s and 1760s Richardson emerged as a leading political figure in the backcountry, regularly representing Prince Frederick's and St. Mark's Parishes in the Commons House of Assembly from 1754 to 1765. In 1768 Richardson was instrumental in negotiating an end to the violent Regulator movement in the backcountry. He was a member of the First and Second Provincial Congresses of South Carolina and was a well-respected militia officer at the start of the Revolutionary War.

In November 1775 Richardson and Colonel William Thomson were given command of 2,500 men and ordered to scatter the large concentration of Loyalists gathering in the South Carolina backcountry. As Richardson and his men advanced through the Loyalist stronghold between the Broad and Saluda Rivers, Loyalists put up brief stands along the way but kept retreating in front of the patriot force. Richardson continued his pursuit, pushing four miles beyond the Cherokee tribal boundary to the Great Cane Break on Reedy River. When he learned that the Tories were encamped there, Richardson sent Thomson to attack them. On December 22, 1775, a sharp fight ensued after the rebels nearly surrounded the Tories. Although the Tory leader Patrick Cunningham managed to escape, the patriot mission of dispersing the Loyalists had been an unquestionable success. Without a leader to guide them, Loyalist resistance fell apart. After Richardson dismissed his men and started on his march home, a heavy snow fell, lending the nickname "Snow Campaign" to the venture.

The Snow Campaign was Richardson's first and last active duty during the Revolutionary War. He was promoted to brigadier general, but his advanced age led him to resign his commission in late 1779. He was captured by the British at the fall of Charleston in May 1780. After several months of harsh treatment at the hands of his British captors, Richardson died at his home plantation, Big Home, in September 1780, and was buried there. KENDRA DEBANY

Buchanan, John. *The Road to Guilford Courthouse: The American Revolution in the Carolinas.* New York: Wiley, 1997.

Edgar, Walter, and N. Louise Bailey, eds. *Biographical Directory of the South Carolina House of Representatives.* Vol. 2, *The Commons House of Assembly, 1692–1775.* Columbia: University of South Carolina Press, 1977.

Lumpkin, Henry. *From Savannah to Yorktown: The American Revolution in the South.* Columbia: University of South Carolina Press, 1981.

ROYAL COUNCIL. The Royal Council, the linear heir of the council under the Lords Proprietors, was a twelve-man governing board created in 1720 to serve as an adviser to the governor, as a court of appeals, and as an upper house of the legislature. Throughout royal rule, the council was dominated by a relatively equal number of planters, merchants, and lawyer/placemen who were nominated by the governor and approved by the London-based Board of Trade for their wealth, political connections, and willingness to support English policies. Legislative experience was not an important criterion for appointment to the council. Its members served without pay, and its meetings were held irregularly at the call of the governor.

During the first several decades of royal rule, the council enjoyed a significant increase in its political autonomy and authority. Members were no longer subjected to the frequent arbitrary dismissals that they had experienced at the hands of the Lords Proprietors. A series of weak governors who deferred to the council added to its power and independence, allowing it to elect its own president and permitting it to compile a list of men suitable for replacements. The upper house soon likened itself, in both prestige and power, to the English House of Lords. This comparison was flawed, however, for councillors were not members of the hereditary nobility who held their political posts for life. Still, the councillors vigorously and successfully fought encroachments on their authority in the 1740s and 1750s by both the Commons House of Assembly and governors. The council did make one concession in this political power struggle in 1739, however, when it surrendered its claim to amend money bills in exchange for the right to exclude the governor from its legislative sessions. Nevertheless, by the mid-1750s South Carolina's upper house carried considerable power and prestige, a highly unusual circumstance at a time when most colonial councils were becoming political nonentities.

The council's stature dropped precipitously after 1756, however, when Governor William Henry Lyttleton arbitrarily suspended William Wragg from that body for opposing the governor's unwillingness to defend the council's right over partial control of the colonial agent. Wragg's dismissal led to a wave of resignations in the upper house, which quickly gained a reputation for being a "dependent body" whose members were "removable at pleasure." Consequently, most men of fortune found the council a "contemptible" body, and no amount of inducement could persuade them to serve on it. Instead, the English ministry, in an attempt to create an absolutely subservient upper legislative body that would give unwavering support of its measures during the Anglo-American dispute, selected men to the council who were financially dependent on the crown. Generally these appointees were British bureaucrats (placemen) of mediocre abilities who were more interested in upholding the crown's prerogative than preserving the colony's welfare. Their conduct in the council became increasingly counterproductive to effective government. With encouragement from King George III, the placemen-dominated upper house attempted to force the assembly to rescind a £1,500 donation given in 1769 to John Wilkes, an English opponent of the king, by refusing to approve any legislation until the lower house returned the "Wilkes fund" to the provincial treasury. The assembly refused to budge on the issue. This political standoff lasted until February 1775, when the upper house, under enormous political pressure, finally approved a tax bill, the last measure enacted under royal government. For all intents and purposes, though, royal rule had ended in South Carolina in 1770. In its place emerged illegal governing committees organized by leading men increasingly frustrated by the council's obstructionist behavior. Indeed, William Henry Drayton in his "Freeman" letter of 1774 to the Continental Congress listed the decline of the council as one of his seven major grievances against the crown. When America declared its independence from Britain in 1776, these de facto governing bodies enabled South Carolina to make a smooth transition from royal rule to self-government. KEITH KRAWCZYNSKI

Greene, Jack P. "The Role of the Lower Houses of Assembly in Eighteenth-Century Politics." *Journal of Southern History* 27 (November 1961): 451–74.

Krawczynski, Keith. *William Henry Drayton: South Carolina Revolutionary Patriot.* Baton Rouge: Louisiana State University Press, 2001.

Sirmans, M. Eugene. "The South Carolina Royal Council, 1720–1763." *William and Mary Quarterly,* 3d ser., 18 (July 1961): 373–91.

Weir, Robert M. *Colonial South Carolina: A History.* 1983. Reprint, Columbia: University of South Carolina Press, 1997.

RUTLEDGE, EDWARD (1749–1800). Lawyer, governor. Edward Rutledge, the youngest son of Dr. John Rutledge and Sarah Hext, was born on November 23, 1749. He studied law under the direction of his older brother, John, and then continued his studies at the Middle Temple in London. He was admitted to the South Carolina Bar in January 1773. His marriage on March 1, 1774, to Henrietta Middleton produced three children. After Henrietta's death in 1792, he married Mary Shubrick Eveleigh on October 28, 1792.

One of Rutledge's first cases in 1773 involved a successful habeas corpus petition that freed a printer jailed for contempt by the upper house of assembly. The reputation he gained in this politically charged case paved the way for his election to the Continental Congress in 1774. At first he hoped to

Edward Rutledge. Stipple engraving on paper. Courtesy, National Portrait Gallery, Smithsonian Institution.

achieve a settlement with Britain that would preserve colonial rights within the British Empire. Events, particularly the beginning of the war, moved him to support independence in principle by February 1776. In June, however, he opposed a formal declaration of independence because he believed that the colonies should first agree on a confederation and secure foreign aid. But when the final vote in favor of independence came, Rutledge swayed his South Carolina colleagues to support it "for the sake of unanimity." He became the youngest signer of the Declaration of Independence.

Rutledge returned to South Carolina in December 1776 to assume his post as a captain in the Charleston Artillery. He also took his seat in the South Carolina House of Representatives, where he worked with some success for a strong executive, military preparedness, and harsh sanctions against Loyalists. When the British captured Charleston in 1780, Rutledge became a prisoner of war on parole. Later that year he and other Charlestonians were arrested for allegedly plotting to organize resistance, a charge that Rutledge denied. The alleged plotters were held prisoner in St. Augustine, Florida, and their property was sequestered for the support of the British army. His war-time experience left Rutledge with a lasting bitterness toward Britain.

Rutledge was freed in a prisoner exchange in July 1781. The following January he returned to the state House of Representatives, where he served for the next thirteen years and became one of South Carolina's most influential political leaders. Rutledge worked in the 1780s to promote the economic recovery of the state and to maintain the political dominance of Lowcountry gentlemen. Both goals required concessions. A skilled conciliator, Rutledge found those concessions easier to make than did many of his compatriots. He played an important role in the postwar confiscation and amercement of Loyalist property and unsuccessfully opposed removal of the state capital from Charleston to Columbia. He later argued against constitutional revision and then helped to devise limited concessions to the Upcountry that still preserved Lowcountry control in the state constitution of 1790. Rutledge also supported what he considered to be the least objectionable of various plans for paper money and debt relief in order to pacify popular discontent.

As a delegate to the South Carolina ratifying convention in 1788, Rutledge was a leader in supporting ratification of the U.S. Constitution. He moved successfully for the endorsement of proposed constitutional amendments to conciliate the opposition. President George Washington twice asked Rutledge if he would accept appointment to the U.S. Supreme Court in the 1790s and also considered him for secretary of state and minister to France, but Rutledge's personal and family circumstances prevented him from leaving South Carolina. Unable for the same reasons to seek election to Congress, he nevertheless had some influence in national politics because of his ties to national leaders and his power in his state. Rutledge supported Alexander Hamilton's financial program but remained strongly anti-British in foreign affairs. He did not align himself completely with either of the two emerging national political parties during Washington's administration.

Rutledge's long tenure in the South Carolina House of Representatives ended in 1796, when he was elected to the state Senate. There Rutledge worked for military preparedness in the undeclared naval war with France that followed the XYZ Affair. He was now aligned with the Federalist Party, but his freedom from British attachments made him more acceptable to Democratic-Republicans than were most Federalists. Rutledge was elected governor in 1798 and continued to strengthen his state's defenses in that capacity. He died in office during the night of January 23–24, 1800, after suffering a stroke. He was buried in St. Philip's Churchyard, Charleston. JAMES HAW

Clow, Richard Brent. "Edward Rutledge of South Carolina, 1749–1800: Unproclaimed Statesman." Ph.D. diss., University of Georgia, 1976.

Haw, James. *John and Edward Rutledge of South Carolina.* Athens: University of Georgia Press, 1997.

Smith, Dorothy Caroline. "The Revolutionary War Service of Edward Rutledge, 1774–1782." M.A. thesis, University of South Carolina, 1947.

RUTLEDGE, JOHN (ca. 1739–1800). Lawyer, jurist, governor. Rutledge's exact date of birth is unknown. The eldest son of Dr. John Rutledge and Sarah Hext, he studied law with his uncle Andrew Rutledge and with James Parsons in Charleston before attending the Middle Temple in London. Admitted to the South Carolina Bar in 1761, he quickly became one of the most successful attorneys in the colony. On May 1, 1763, he married Elizabeth Grimké. They had ten children, eight of whom survived to adulthood.

Rutledge served in the Commons House of Assembly from 1761 to 1775 and became one of its leaders. He upheld the rights of the "country" in a series of disputes with successive royal governors and firmly opposed the Stamp, Townshend, and Tea Acts, representing his colony at the Stamp Act Congress in 1765. As a delegate to the First and Second Continental Congresses, he advocated a steadfast defense of American rights, but by means that would not impede reconciliation with the mother country. When events made reconciliation impossible, he reluctantly accepted independence as a necessity.

In the meantime, as royal authority dissolved in his own and other colonies, Rutledge supported a congressional resolution for the creation of new governments based on constitutions created by the people, not royal charters, until the crisis was resolved. He left Congress in November 1775 to carry that resolution to South Carolina. Rutledge was one of the drafters of the state constitution of 1776 and was elected president (governor) of South Carolina in March of the same year. Under his energetic leadership, the new state repulsed a British attack on Charleston in June 1776 and suppressed a Cherokee uprising later that summer.

Rutledge resigned as president in March 1778 to protest the adoption of a new state constitution of which he disapproved, but he was elected governor under that constitution in February 1779. When the British captured Charleston and overran South Carolina in 1780, Rutledge escaped to function as a one-man government in exile. He twice visited Philadelphia to seek increased aid for the South from Congress but spent most of his time with the southern Continental army organizing and trying to supply his state's militia for continued resistance. Eventual military successes in the South allowed him to restore state government and turn over the governorship to his elected successor, John Mathewes, in January 1782.

After serving again in Congress from 1782 to 1783, Rutledge accepted appointment to the South Carolina Court of Chancery, and he remained a leader in the state legislature in the 1780s. His experience in Congress

John Rutledge. Oil on mahogany panel. Courtesy, National Portrait Gallery, Smithsonian Institution.

convinced him that the United States needed a stronger central government. He was chosen as one of South Carolina's delegates to the constitutional convention in 1787.

Rutledge played a prominent role in writing the federal Constitution. He advocated a national government of greatly increased but still limited powers and entrusted to an executive and a Congress designed to consist of gentlemen made relatively independent of public opinion. As chairman of the committee of detail, he had a major role in the enumeration of congressional powers, the provision forbidding taxation of exports, and the ban on national prohibition of slave imports until 1808. Rutledge also promoted the constitution's adoption as a member of the South Carolina ratifying convention.

In 1789 Rutledge reluctantly accepted appointment as one of the first justices of the United States Supreme Court. He resigned from that position in 1791 to become chief justice of South Carolina, an office he held until 1795. Since the Supreme Court was just getting organized during his tenure, he made no important rulings on the federal bench.

In the early 1790s John Rutledge became an emotionally troubled man. Large debts threatened the loss of all of his property. A serious illness in 1781, coupled with gout, had severely damaged his health. His wife's sudden death in 1792 was the final blow, plunging him into deep depression.

Apparently unaware of Rutledge's problems, President George Washington appointed him chief justice of the United States Supreme Court in 1795. However, before learning of his nomination, Rutledge made a speech denouncing the recently negotiated Jay Treaty with Britain. This speech outraged Federalists and, combined with reports of his "derangement" and financial problems, caused the Federalist-dominated Senate to reject his nomination. Probably before hearing of the rejection, a despondent Rutledge attempted suicide and then resigned from the South Carolina Supreme Court for reasons of health. Except for one term in the South Carolina House of Representatives, Rutledge remained in retirement until his death on July 18, 1800. JAMES HAW

Haw, James. *John and Edward Rutledge of South Carolina*. Athens: University of Georgia Press, 1997.

SALVADOR, FRANCIS (ca. 1747–1776). Legislator, patriot. Salvador was born in London, son of the wealthy merchant Jacob Salvador. Members of the prominent Sephardic Salvador family left Portugal in the late seventeenth century after the Inquisition, settling first in Holland and then in England, where they became one of the country's wealthiest Jewish families. After he had been educated on the Continent, the family lost its fortune with the failure of the Dutch East India Company. The family coat of arms is in the possession of the College of Charleston.

Salvador came to South Carolina in an attempt to restore the family fortune, arriving in Charleston on December 6, 1773. His indigo plantation in Ninety Six District along Coronaca Creek, known as Corn Acre, was the remnant of more than 200,000 acres that had been acquired earlier by his uncle and father-in-law, Joseph Salvador. That property covered more than half of present-day Greenwood County and until the 1920s was often called "Jews Lands." He acquired roughly thirty slaves and with his social polish quickly made friends and won acceptance among the leading planters in this Upcountry region.

In the events leading to the Revolutionary War, Salvador quickly identified with the patriot cause. Its leaders, impressed with his education and ability, accepted him into their ranks. Slightly over a year after arriving in Charleston, he was elected on December 19, 1774, to the First Provincial Congress of South Carolina, along with Patrick Calhoun and eight other representatives from Ninety Six District. Salvador was the first person of the Jewish faith elected to the South Carolina legislature, while the Jewish historian Barnett Elzas claimed that he was "the first Jew in America to represent the masses in a popular assembly."

Salvador served on important committees for the First and Second Provincial Congresses and for South Carolina's first General Assembly. On August 1, 1776, he died during an official mission aimed at consolidating backcountry support. A force of Cherokee Indians and Loyalists ambushed his unit at night. Salvador died after being shot and scalped. His death three weeks after the signing of the Declaration of Independence made him the first Jew to die for the patriot cause. Chief Justice William Henry Drayton of the South Carolina Supreme Court wrote in his memoirs that Salvador's death "excited universal regret. . . . His manners were those of a polished gentleman." In 1950 a plaque in Charleston's City Hall Park was dedicated to his memory. JACK BASS

Elzas, Barnett A. *The Jews of South Carolina from the Earliest Times to the Present Day.* 1905. Reprint, Spartanburg, S.C.: Reprint Company, 1972.
Herd, E. Don, Jr. *The South Carolina Upcountry: Historical and Biographical Sketches.* Vol. 1. Greenwood, S.C.: Attic Press, 1981.

SOUTH CAROLINA. Warship. At the beginning of the Revolutionary War, patriot leaders of South Carolina worried about threats from the sea. Local officials dealt with this problem by creating a state navy—the most famous component of which was the frigate *South Carolina,* the largest warship under American command during the war. The ship was 168 feet long and 47 feet wide, sported forty guns, and carried 550 men. To obtain such a ship, the state sent Commodore Alexander Gillon to Europe in 1778. A successful merchant, Gillon spoke fluent French and Dutch, had extensive sea experience, and possessed marriage ties to influential Charleston families.

Surplus warships were scarce, but a nearly completed French frigate called *L'Indien* existed in Amsterdam. Through personal connections, Gillon secured a three-year lease of the ship in 1780 but did not get to sea until August 1781. The *South Carolina* arrived off Charleston in December, only to find the city occupied by the British. The commodore then took the ship south to Havana, where he received supplies from the Spanish government. In return, Gillon assisted the captain-general of Havana in capturing New Providence in the Bahamas in May 1782. After a dispute among allies over the spoils of war, the frigate headed north to Philadelphia. The *South Carolina* was refitted during autumn 1782 and left on her second cruise in

December, only to fall captive to three British cruisers at the mouth of the Delaware River.

Since the *South Carolina* failed to benefit Gillon's state, the frigate generated considerable controversy. Some questioned as impracticable the idea of defending the state's coast. Many challenged the choice of Gillon to command, particularly since John Paul Jones also wanted the frigate. Most telling of all, the mass of confusing debts generated by the ship remained unsettled until 1856 and clouded the reputation of all tied to the enterprise. JAMES A. LEWIS

Grimball, Berkeley. "Commodore Alexander Gillon, South Carolina, 1741–1794." Master's thesis, Duke University, 1951.

Lewis, James A. *The Final Campaign of the American Revolution: Rise and Fall of the Spanish Bahamas.* Columbia: University of South Carolina Press, 1991.

———. *Neptune's Militia: The Frigate* South Carolina *during the American Revolution.* Kent, Ohio: Kent State University Press, 1999.

Middlebrook, Louis E. *The Frigate "South Carolina": A Famous Revolutionary War Ship.* Salem, Mass.: Essex Institute, 1929.

Smith, D. E. Huger. "Commodore Alexander Gillon and the Frigate South Carolina." *South Carolina Historical and Genealogical Magazine* 9 (October 1908): 189–219.

STATE FLAG. South Carolina's blue flag with its white crescent rising above the white palmetto tree is simple in design but profoundly symbolic of a long history. Born for practicality, South Carolina's first state flag was a signal device used in the opening days of the Revolutionary War. In 1776 the Council of Safety ordered Colonel William Moultrie to produce a signal flag and supplied blue cloth for that purpose. Moultrie used the silver crescent worn on his troop's hats, placing this device in the upper-corner flagstaff side on the blue cloth.

This flag signaled victory to Charleston following Moultrie's repulse of the British fleet from the hastily erected palmetto log fort on Sullivan's Island. The palmetto tree immediately became a popular symbol. Though not incorporated into the flag during the Revolution, the palmetto tree did become part of the new state seal, firmly establishing it as a state emblem.

The Palmetto Regiment, South Carolina's volunteer unit raised for Mexican War duty in 1846, carried a banner of blue. These colors were the first American banners to be raised over Mexico City upon its capture. After the war, a medal presented to the regimental veterans clearly depicted this flag with a palmetto tree in the center of an oval.

In December 1860, when South Carolina seceded from the Union, Representative Plowden C. J. Weston called for the appointment of a joint committee to devise a South Carolina national flag or ensign. Exactly one month later the committee introduced a resolution creating a white flag with a green palmetto tree in the center and a blue union with a white crescent. Representative Robert Barnwell Rhett, Jr., amended the resolution to read "the National Flag or Ensign of South Carolina shall be blue with a white palmetto tree upright thereon, and a white crescent in the upper corner." Rhett reasoned that the colonial flag of blue with a white crescent and the white palmetto tree addition created a simple, beautiful flag. Not all of the legislators agreed with Rhett, however, and for seven days debate occurred in the House, the Senate, and the newspapers. Finally, on January 28, 1861, Rhett's design was approved, and the blue flag with a white palmetto tree centered and a white crescent with horns pointing upward in the corner became the official state flag. In April, when Fort Sumter was taken, this flag flew beside the flag of the Confederacy.

In 1869 the Reconstruction government raised the flag issue again. A resolution passed by the General Assembly provided that a United States flag and the 1861 state flag would wave over the State House. Thirty years later the legislature hotly debated the proposal of changing the flag's color from blue to purple to symbolize the blue flag being soaked with gallant South Carolina red blood. This gesture to honor the Confederate dead and the "Lost Cause" was overwhelmingly defeated; the flag remained blue.

In 1906 Senator Benjamin R. Tillman suggested that the state's coat of arms be incorporated with two shields leaning against the palmetto tree's base. Alexander Salley, secretary of the Historical Commission, quickly pointed out that the flag adhered to statutory law. Following the statutes, Salley and Governor Martin F. Ansel produced a lovely state flag in honor of President William Howard Taft's 1909 visit to the state. This effort spurred the passage of a 1910 General Assembly act providing for the display of the flag over public buildings. Clemson College was directed to manufacture the flags as prescribed by an 1861 General Assembly resolution. The act also stipulated that the secretary of the Historical Commission approve the design, so Salley carefully supervised every detail, even selecting the shade of blue. The only major change made was to place the crescent closer to the flagstaff with the horns turned to the staff rather than upward.

Manufactured by commercial firms in the twenty-first century, the state flag has changed little since 1910. With its simple design and long history, the flag has been an outstanding representation of South Carolina. ROBERTA V. H. COPP

Wates, Wylma A. *A Flag Worthy of Your State and People: The History of the South Carolina State Flag.* 2d ed. Columbia: South Carolina Department of Archives and History, 1996.

STATE MOTTOES. South Carolina has two official mottoes. These were engraved on the original great seal in 1777. ANIMIS OPIBUSQUE PARATI (Prepared in Mind and Resources) is on the rim of the seal obverse (front), accompanying a picture of a palmetto tree. The motto had earlier appeared on a £50 South Carolina banknote issued in 1776. The words were taken from the second book of Virgil's *Aeneid,* at the point in the story where Aeneas joined his band of followers who had escaped from the burning city of Troy and had gathered on the beach. Aeneas said that he found his Trojans armed, equipped, ready, and willing to follow him into exile. They were about to set forth on the great voyage of adventure that would ultimately lead to the founding of Rome. Revolutionary South Carolina's use of this motto expressed confidence in the state's destiny.

DUM SPIRO SPERO (While I Breathe, I Hope) appeared on the reverse (back) of the great seal, along with an image of the Roman goddess Spes (Hope). The phrase was popular in the British Isles, where it was borne as a motto by over fifty families. It had also been used as a personal motto by King Charles I and appeared on coins he minted during the English civil war. The words were probably chosen for South Carolina's seal as an expression of optimism that fit well with the picture of Hope. No special connection with Charles I or any of the various families that employed the motto is known. DAVID C. R. HEISSER

Heisser, David C. R. *The State Seal of South Carolina: A Short History.* Columbia: South Carolina Department of Archives and History, 1992.

Pinches, Rosemary, ed. *Elvin's Handbook of Mottoes.* Rev. ed. London: Heraldry Today, 1971.

STATE SEAL. The great seal of South Carolina was first used on a document dated May 22, 1777. It was a double-sided, circular device impressed on wax and appended to documents by cords or ribbons. Its principal designers were William Henry Drayton and Arthur Middleton. Drayton was mainly responsible for the design of the obverse (front), and Middleton for the reverse (back).

The inspiration for the design came from the Battle of Sullivan's Island, June 28, 1776, when troops under Colonel William Moultrie, manning a palmetto-log fort, defeated a Royal Navy squadron. The seal obverse showed

The silver matrix for the state seal. Courtesy, South Carolina
Department of Archives and History.

a palmetto on the shore representing the fort, at the base of which was a
blasted oak representing the oak-timbered ships. From the tree hung shields
inscribed "March 26," the date of ratification of the state constitution in 1776,
and "July 4," for the Declaration of Independence. Twelve spears representing the sister states were bound to the palmetto's trunk by a ribbon. In the
palm hung with shields, the seal's designers chose an ancient Roman emblem
of victory. The reverse depicted the Roman goddess Spes (Hope) walking on
the beach at dawn over discarded weapons and holding a laurel blossom.
Spes symbolized the patriots' optimism. The two state mottoes appeared on
the seal.

The original pendant seal was cumbersome to make and affix to documents, so sometime in the mid-1780s a small, one-sided seal with the pic-
tures from the great seal compressed into ovals was introduced. Small seals
have mostly been used ever since. The original great seal was used for the last
time on the Ordinance of Secession (1860).

The state also uses a picture of the two faces of the great seal in ovals on
a grassy compartment. On the viewer's left is the goddess Liberty in a long
flowing gown bearing a *pileus,* or cap of freedom, on a spear. She holds a
wreath of laurel in her outstretched left hand. On the right is an army officer of the Revolutionary War with a tricorn hat and a sword. Overhead
the winged figure of Fame emerges from the clouds. She blows one trumpet
and carries another. The design first appeared on the nameplate of the *State*

Gazette of South Carolina in 1785. The identity of the designer is unknown, and the emblem was not adopted in any legislative enactment. Tradition, however, calls the design the coat of arms, and it frequently decorates state publications and stationery. DAVID C. R. HEISSER

Heisser, David C. R. *The State Seal of South Carolina: A Short History.* Columbia: South Carolina Department of Archives and History, 1992.
Salley, Alexander S., Jr. *The Seal of the State of South Carolina.* Columbia, S.C.: State Company, 1907.
Seals and Symbols of South Carolina Government through Three Centuries. Columbia, S.C.: Columbia Museums of Art and Science, 1982.

STUART, JOHN (1718–1779). Soldier, colonial official. Stuart was born on September 25, 1718, in Inverness, Scotland, the son of John and Christian Stuart. As a youth, he joined the Royal Navy, and his ship circumnavigated the globe between 1740 and 1744. By 1748 Stuart had amassed sufficient capital to relocate to Britain's North American colonies, and he eventually settled in Charleston. During his time in South Carolina, he served as a fire master, a tax assessor, and an assemblyman. As a militia captain, in 1759 Stuart was assigned to Fort Loudoun in East Tennessee among the Overhill Cherokees, and he was the only officer spared following the capitulation of the fort to the Cherokees in August 1760.

Having gained notoriety by his escape, Stuart was named superintendent of Indian affairs for the Southern District by General Edward Braddock in January 1762. At first Stuart operated out of Charleston. His initial job was to familiarize the southern Indians with the Proclamation Line of 1763, which was supposed to keep English settlers east of the Appalachian Mountains. Stuart met with leaders of the various tribes at Augusta, Georgia, in December 1763. The Treaty of Augusta both recognized the eastern boundary of the Cherokees and established a 225-square-mile reservation for the Catawbas.

In response to the unfair practices employed in the highly competitive Indian trade, Stuart pursued policies designed to promote Anglo-Indian stability. Stuart's new position and authority placed both the licensure of Indian traders and the transfer of Indian lands under his control, superceding four decades of control by South Carolina's colonial government. Some officials complained about Stuart's enlarged powers. Thomas Boone, governor of South Carolina, wrote to the Board of Trade in 1764 with the suggestion that Stuart should be made subordinate to the governor and council of each colony. The biographer J. Russell Snapp noted that Stuart's Indian policies, often made at the expense of profitable trade or land acquisition, insured that colonial Americans and their British rulers would eventually clash.

The advent of the Revolutionary War made Stuart's job more difficult. The Charleston Sons of Liberty suspected that Stuart, a Loyalist, opposed their agenda and was using the southern tribes against patriots as early as the summer of 1775. Carolina patriots forced Stuart out of his Charleston base to Florida, although they kept his family as hostages to ensure Stuart's good behavior.

During the war, the patriots organized their own Indian agents, one of which, George Galphin, came into conflict with Stuart regularly. In the fall of 1775 Galphin met with Creeks and told them that their friend John Stuart was old and sick and could not be counted on by them for much longer. By late 1775 Stuart authorized his own Indian agents to treat patriot agents such as Galphin as rebels and to arrest them when possible. He also began organizing Indian tribes for war, an action that solidified opposition to the British and further escalated the conflict in the southern interior. But Stuart did not live to see the end of the war. He died on March 21, 1779, in Pensacola, West Florida. MICHAEL P. MORRIS

Alden, John Richard. *John Stuart and the Southern Colonial Frontier: A Study of Indian Relations, War, Trade, and Land Problems in the Southern Wilderness, 1754–1775.* 1944. Reprint, New York: Gordian, 1966.

Snapp, J. Russell. *John Stuart and the Struggle for Empire on the Southern Frontier.* Baton Rouge: Louisiana State University Press, 1996.

SULLIVAN'S ISLAND, BATTLE OF (June 28, 1776). The Battle of Sullivan's Island was the first major patriot victory in the Revolutionary War. In February 1776, after British plans to capture Charleston were revealed, South Carolina patriots began construction of a fort on Sullivan's Island close to the main shipping channel at the mouth of Charleston harbor. Colonel William Moultrie was given command of the island's forces and ordered to supervise the fort's construction.

The unnamed fort was to be a square with five-hundred-footlong walls and a bastion at each corner. It was built of thousands of palmetto trees cut to make two parallel log walls sixteen feet apart and more than ten feet high. The space between the walls was filled with sand. By late June only the two walls and bastions facing the channel were complete thirty-one cannons were in place, and fewer than four hundred soldiers garrisoned the incomplete fort. At the other end of Sullivan's Island, three hundred soldiers were positioned at Breach Inlet to block the British from crossing from Long Island (Isle of Palms) and attacking the fort from the rear.

A British fleet, which arrived on June 1, included nine men-of-war mounting almost three hundred cannons. On June 8 a British surrender demand was rejected, and the next day British infantrymen landed on Long Island. On June 28 the British ships advanced to attack the Sullivan's Island fort. By 11:30 A.M. six warships were in position and opened fire. The fort's guns soon responded. Not long after the bombardment began, three more British warships attempted to move into position between Sullivan's Island and the mainland, fire into the fort's unprotected rear, and block patriot troops from reinforcing the fort. But the movement failed when all three ran aground on the sandbanks in the harbor's mouth. Two later freed themselves, while the third remained hard aground.

The bombardment continued into the evening, but the fort withstood the pounding from the British heavy guns. Its palmetto-log and sand walls absorbed the solid shot and shells, resulting in little structural damage. At the same time, patriot rounds tore into the wooden warships. During the afternoon when the British on Long Island attempted to cross Breach Inlet, patriots on Sullivan's Island were able to turn them back.

At 9:00 P.M. the British ceased their attack and pulled out of the fort's range. Several warships had been damaged, and more than two hundred sailors were casualties. Inside the fort fewer than forty patriots had suffered the same fate. The next day the British set the grounded ship on fire, which exploded when the flames reached the powder magazine. The British soon withdrew, leaving Charleston free from attack until 1780.

Shortly after the battle, the fort was named Fort Moultrie in honor of its commander. Fort Moultrie is administered as part of Fort Sumter National Monument, a unit of the National Park Service. RICHARD W. HATCHER III

Stokeley, Jim. *Fort Moultrie: Constant Defender.* Washington, D.C.: Department of the Interior, 1985.

SUMTER, THOMAS (1734–1832). Soldier, congressman, U.S. senator. Sumter was born on August 14, 1734, in Hanover County, Virginia. His father, William, was a miller and former indentured servant, while his mother, Patience, was a midwife. Most of Thomas Sumter's early years were spent tending livestock and helping his father at the mill, not in school. He joined the provincial militia at the outbreak of the French and Indian War and rose to the rank of sergeant. In 1761 Sumter was selected to participate in a diplomatic mission to the Cherokee nation and escorted an Indian delegation to London the following year. After returning to Virginia via Charleston, he was imprisoned for indebtedness but escaped and fled to South Carolina. Around 1764 Sumter settled in St. John's Berkeley Parish near the Santee River (Orangeburg County) and opened a country store. The mercantile venture prospered, and Sumter soon owned considerable property. In 1767 he married Mary Cantey Jameson, a wealthy, crippled widow eleven years his senior. Sumter and his wife moved to her plantation, Great Savannah, across the Santee in St. Mark's Parish. The couple had two children.

The Revolutionary War interrupted Sumter's comfortable life, and he found himself again a soldier. After being elected a delegate to the First and Second Provincial Congresses, Sumter participated in the Snow Campaign (December 1775), the Battle of Fort Moultrie (June 28, 1776), the Cherokee campaign (July–October 1776), and engagements in Georgia (1777, 1778). On September 19, 1778, Sumter left the army with the rank of colonel and returned to private life. He was in retirement when the British captured Charleston in May 1780. It was during this stage of the war, when the patriot tide in the state was at its lowest ebb, that Sumter made his greatest mark.

With South Carolina apparently subdued, the British were poised to push north and end the war in short order. They raided and burned Sumter's home in May 1780, an attack that Sumter took personally. He immediately returned to the field and organized local militiamen into an army of backcountry partisans who informally elected him their general. In the summer of 1780 "Sumter's Brigade" was the only organized opposition to the British in South Carolina. Though the brigade met with mixed success in engagements at Rocky Mount (July 30, 1780), Hanging Rock (August 6, 1780), and Fishing Creek (August 18, 1780), Sumter's exploits in the upper part of the state injected beleaguered South Carolina patriots with a renewed energy to resist, earning Sumter the nickname "Gamecock" for his daring and tenacious resistance. After four months of invaluable but unofficial service, Sumter was commissioned as a brigadier general of the South Carolina militia on October 6, 1780. His force fought well at Fishdam Ford (November 9, 1780) and Blackstock's (November 20, 1780), where Sumter was severely wounded. Incapacitated for several months, he returned to action in February 1781 and led his troops in additional encounters at Fort Granby (February 19–21, May 15, 1781) and Orangeburg (May 10–11, 1781).

Sumter's pride and rash manner made him ill-suited to accept command from others. When the Continental army returned to South Carolina in the spring of 1781, Sumter was less than cooperative with General Nathanael

Thomas Sumter. Ink Wash on illustration board. Courtesy, National Portrait Gallery, Smithsonian Institution.

Greene. Sumter attempted to resign as early as May 1781, but Greene refused to allow it. Maintaining his independent command, Sumter finally joined Greene in July 1781 and led "the raid of the dog days" into the Lowcountry. Still smarting over command changes and militia reorganization, Sumter resigned in February 1782 and closed his military career.

The remainder of Sumter's public life was spent in politics. He served eight terms in the General Assembly between 1776 and 1790. In 1783 he helped found the town of Stateburg, which he promoted for the new state capital. Elected by Camden District to the U.S. House of Representatives, he served five terms in Congress between 1789 and 1801. Sumter resigned from Congress on December 15, 1801, upon learning of his election to the U.S. Senate, where he served until December 16, 1810. In Washington, Sumter was a staunch Jeffersonian who remained devoted to the backcountry republican values he had known since childhood. Sumter died on June 1, 1832, at the age of ninety-seven. He was the last surviving general of the Revolutionary War. Sumter County and Fort Sumter were named in his honor. MATTHEW A. LOCKHART

Bass, Robert D. *Gamecock: The Life and Campaigns of General Thomas Sumter.* New York: Holt, Rinehart and Winston, 1961.

Gregorie, Anne King. *History of Sumter County.* Sumter, S.C.: Library Board of Sumter County, 1954.

———. *Thomas Sumter.* Columbia, S.C.: R. L. Bryan, 1931.

TARLETON, BANASTRE (1754–1833). British soldier. Few other figures in South Carolina history have been labeled as villainous as Banastre Tarleton has. He was born in Liverpool, England, on August 21, 1754, the third child of John Tarleton and Jane Parker.

Banastre Tarleton. Engraving, 1782. Library of Congress, Rare Book and Special Collections Division.

John Tarleton, who served as mayor of Liverpool, wished for the popular and athletic Banastre to study law and enrolled him at Oxford. When his father died in 1773, Banastre first used the legacy he received to further his study of the law, but on April 20, 1775, he purchased a cornet's commission in the First Dragoon Guards.

Tarleton sailed for America in February 1776 and was part of the British force that attacked Charleston in June 1776, although he played no major role in operations against the fort on Sullivan's Island. In the northern theater, Tarleton served with Lieutenant Colonel William Harcourt of the Sixteenth Regiment of Light Dragoons and played a key role in the capture of General Charles Lee in December 1776. Impressing his superior officers, Tarleton rose steadily through the ranks, and on August 1, 1778, he was appointed lieutenant colonel of Lord Cathcart's Legion, a mixed unit of cavalry and infantry comprised primarily of Loyalists. Tarleton led this unit, which was usually referred to as the British Legion or simply the Legion, when it sailed from New York southward in December 1779. Most of the British cavalry horses perished in the long and stormy voyage from New York to Georgia, so General Sir Henry Clinton sent Tarleton and his dragoons to the Beaufort area to collect new mounts. Tarleton shined in the ensuing Charleston campaign. His dragoons completely overwhelmed the American cavalry at

Biggin's Bridge near Moncks Corner on April 14, 1780, and then surprised and beat them again at Lenud's Ferry on the Santee River on May 6.

Tarleton gained his greatest notoriety in the aftermath of Charleston's surrender. Lord Cornwallis dispatched his Legion to overtake Colonel Abraham Buford and the last remaining detachment of Continental troops in South Carolina after Charleston's fall. Aware of the British pursuit, Buford retreated toward North Carolina. Covering 105 miles in fifty-four hours, Tarleton's force caught up with the Americans on May 29, 1780, at the Waxhaws (near the North Carolina / South Carolina border in modern-day Lancaster County). Tarleton's cavalry smashed through Buford's infantry, and slaughter then ensued. In the charge, Tarleton's horse was shot out from under him. According to Tarleton, his men, believing they had lost their commander, were "stimulated . . . to a vindictive asperity not easily restrained." His dragoons cut down men with their sabers as those soldiers tried to surrender or run away. Tarleton reported that 113 American soldiers "were killed on the spot" while 150 others were so badly wounded that Tarleton had to leave them behind on parole. The British had only 5 killed and 14 wounded. Word of the massacre spread quickly. The action at the Waxhaws established Tarleton as a ruthless and bloodthirsty villain in the minds of South Carolina patriots, and the phrase "Tarleton's quarter" came to mean "no quarter."

Following the American defeat at Camden, Tarleton's dragoons again chased down fleeing soldiers. On August 18, 1780, he surprised and routed a detachment under General Thomas Sumter at Fishing Creek. At Blackstock's plantation on November 20, 1780, Tarleton again attacked Sumter, but this time Sumter held a strong fortified position from which his men inflicted over one hundred casualties upon the British troops. Both sides claimed victory in the action. Tarleton also had troubles with Francis Marion. Ordered by Cornwallis to "get at Mr. Marion," Tarleton pursued his force through the swamps of the Pee Dee region but was unable to catch him. At the Battle of Cowpens (January 17, 1781), Tarleton suffered one of the most critical defeats of the Revolutionary War when his troops crumbled before the ragtag army of General Daniel Morgan. It was Tarleton's last hurrah in South Carolina. In the wake of the defeat, General Cornwallis determined to drive Nathanael Greene into North Carolina; Tarleton and the Legion went with him. In March 1781 Tarleton fought in the Battle of Guilford Courthouse, North Carolina, where an American musket ball mangled his right hand, and he was captured with the British army at Yorktown.

After the war Tarleton returned to England and served in Parliament. He died on January 16, 1833, and was buried in the churchyard at Leintwardine,

England. While portrayed by many historians as cruel and inhumane, one cannot deny Tarleton his success. He excelled at quick-strike, surprise attacks that overwhelmed his enemy. Until Blackstock's and Cowpens, his methods were brutally effective against South Carolina patriots. CARL BORICK

Bass, Robert D. *The Green Dragoon: The Lives of Banastre Tarleton and Mary Robinson.* New York: Holt, 1957.

Pancake, John S. *This Destructive War: The British Campaign in the Carolinas, 1780–1782.* University: University of Alabama Press, 1985.

Tarleton, Banastre. *A History of the Campaigns of 1780 and 1781, in the Southern Provinces of North America.* 1787. Reprint, Spartanburg, S.C.: Reprint Company, 1967.

TIMOTHY, PETER (ca. 1725–1782). Newspaper printer, patriot. Timothy was born in Holland to Louis and Elizabeth Timothée before they immigrated to Philadelphia in 1731 and anglicized their name to Timothy. His father was a business partner of Benjamin Franklin, and in 1733 Lewis Timothy settled in Charleston and became printer of the *South-Carolina Gazette.* After his father's death in 1738, Peter's mother, Elizabeth, continued the contract. In 1739 Elizabeth bought out Franklin's interest in the partnership for her son. By 1746 Peter reached his legal majority and assumed the family business. The previous year, on December 8, 1745, he married Ann Donavan. The marriage produced at least twelve children.

Peter Timothy was the official printer to the Commons House of Assembly and maintained a monopoly on the South Carolina printing business until 1758, when Robert Wells began publishing the *South-Carolina Weekly Gazette.* Timothy became postmaster general for Charleston in 1756, and during the Stamp Act Crisis he became deputy postmaster of the southern colonies and acting postmaster of the district in 1766. The *South-Carolina Gazette* under Timothy became increasingly partisan in the colonial crisis. It published critiques of Governor James Glen, expressed support of the Wilkes Fund and American manufactures, and roundly condemned the Boston Massacre and the blockade of the port of Boston.

Timothy's interests extended beyond printing. He was elected to the Twentieth Royal Assembly (1751–1754) by St. Peter's Parish. Active in the Sons of Liberty, he was a member of the General Committee of Correspondence in 1774 and chairman of the Committee of Observation and clerk of the Council of Safety in 1775. He served on the Committee of Ninety-Nine for Charleston and in the First and Second Provincial Congresses (1775–1776) for St. Philip's and St. Michael's Parishes. In 1776 the House elected him clerk of the First General Assembly. He offered to resign when members protested his dual office holding and yet was retained. Timothy was also secretary of the Grand Lodge of Free Masons, a founding member of the Charleston Library Society, a member of the South Carolina Society, a pewholder in St. Philip's Church, and a landholder in Orangeburg and Berkeley Counties.

Timothy was an ardent patriot. During the siege of Charleston, he was a military observer and watched the British fleet from atop St. Michael's steeple. Following the fall of Charleston in May 1780, Timothy refused to take a loyalty oath and was exiled to St. Augustine with other prominent city patriots. After a ten-month imprisonment he was exchanged but forbidden to return to Charleston. Reunited with family in Philadelphia, Timothy in autumn 1782 accompanied two daughters and a grandchild on a ship bound for the West Indies. Intending to visit his daughter in Antigua, and perhaps plot a return to South Carolina, Timothy and some members of his family perished in a storm off the coast of Delaware. His will, proved on May 2, 1783, left all his property to his wife, an unmarried daughter named Sarah, his invalid son Robert, and his son Benjamin Franklin, who would eventually continue the family printing enterprise after his mother's death. MARTHA J. KING

Cohen, Hennig. *The South Carolina Gazette, 1732–1775.* Columbia: University of South Carolina Press, 1953.

Edgar, Walter, and N. Louise Bailey, eds. *Biographical Directory of the South Carolina House of Representatives.* Vol. 2, *The Commons House of Assembly, 1692–1775.* Columbia: University of South Carolina Press, 1977.

McMurtrie, Douglas C. "The Correspondence of Peter Timothy, Printer of Charlestown, with Benjamin Franklin." *South Carolina Historical and Genealogical Magazine* 35 (October 1934): 123–29.

VANDERHORST, ARNOLDUS (1748–1815). Governor. Vanderhorst, the son of Arnoldus Vanderhorst and Elizabeth Simons, was born on March 21, 1748, in Christ Church Parish. He wed Elizabeth Raven on March 5, 1771, and the union produced at least six children. A successful planter and slaveholder, Vanderhorst owned a 1,350-acre plantation on Kiawah Island as well as substantial landholdings elsewhere in South Carolina.

Vanderhorst's public career began in 1772 when he was elected to the Thirtieth Royal Assembly by Christ Church Parish. He was reelected three times before that body was dissolved in 1775. As the Revolutionary War approached, he demonstrated his patriotic sympathies by serving on the Committee of Ninety-Nine (1774) and representing his home parish in the First (1775) and Second (1775–1776) Provincial Congresses. During the war,

Vanderhorst served as a militia captain at Haddrell's Point (1776) and as a colonel under General Francis Marion (1782).

Following the war, Vanderhorst spent most of his time in Charleston. He operated a mercantile firm and came to own considerable property around the city. He also became an active figure in civic affairs, serving twice as intendant mayor for Charleston (1785–1786, 1791) and as a trustee for the College of Charleston (1785–1791). Still a landowner in Christ Church, he represented that parish in the General Assembly nine times between 1776 and 1794, twice in the House and seven times in the Senate. Aligning himself with Charleston's strong Federalist contingent, Vanderhorst joined his Lowcountry colleagues in resisting Upcountry demands for legislative reapportionment and opposing the relocation of the capital from Charleston to Columbia, which he sarcastically dubbed "Town of Refuge," believing that the remote inland location would make the new capital a haven for outlaws.

Vanderhorst's Federalist connections, particularly the powerful Rutledge-Pinckney faction, led to his election as governor on December 17, 1794. Although serving as governor of a state rife with sectionalism and partisanship, Vanderhorst managed to set aside his personal biases and provide South Carolina with positive leadership. He requested improvement of state jail facilities and sought revision of the criminal code, proposing "instead of the indiscriminate punishment of death . . . inflict a long or short term of solitary confinement on the offenders, in some measure proportionate to their crime." An advocate of public education, Vanderhorst urged the General Assembly to establish schools throughout the state to diffuse "knowledge and information" so that "morals and virtue" might "adorn and characterize the citizens of South Carolina." Also, with Indian troubles in the West and the threat of war with Britain and France looming over the state and nation, Vanderhorst pushed the state to attend to its defenses, placing a priority on the protection of both Charleston and the frontier. At the close of his term as governor in 1796, Vanderhorst still held his party's favor and was selected to act as a presidential elector for John Adams.

Following his gubernatorial term, Vanderhorst served a final term in the House as a representative for St. Philip's and St. Michael's Parishes (1798–1799). He died in Charleston on January 29, 1815, and was buried in St. Michael's Churchyard. MATTHEW A. LOCKHART

Bailey, N. Louise, Mary L. Morgan, and Carolyn R. Taylor, eds. *Biographical Directory of the South Carolina Senate, 1776–1985.* 3 vols. Columbia: University of South Carolina Press, 1986.

WALTER, THOMAS (ca. 1740–1789). Botanist, planter, patriot, politician. Walter was probably born in Hampshire, England. His aunt Frances Knight died there in 1784. She left a house to Walter from which he received rents until his death. His parents' names, his place and time of birth, and his education are not known. By 1769 Walter was in Charleston and remained in the Lowcountry for the next twenty years. He acquired 4,500 acres through purchase and royal grants.

During this period Walter produced a manuscript for *Flora Caroliniana* that stands as a hallmark in its genre. It was the first flora document of a region of North America to utilize the Linnaean system of classification. For years Walter had collected plants in the coastal plain of South Carolina and cultivated many in his garden. He also received many specimens from the plant collector John Fraser. Fraser, a Scot, had traveled to South Carolina and, after meeting Walter, agreed to collect plants in the Piedmont and foothills for him. Walter added four hundred plants from Fraser to his own collection of approximately six hundred. His Latin descriptions of these species became the basis for the *Flora*. More than one thousand species are described, many of which were new to science, including Walter's pine (*Pinus glabra*) from the coastal plain and a magnolia (*Magnolia fraseri*) from the Carolina mountains that Walter named for Fraser. The plant collections, along with Walter's manuscript, were taken by Fraser to London in 1788. The *Flora* was published that year, and the collection remains housed in the British Museum of Natural History.

Walter collected plants and wrote descriptions while operating as a merchant and planter in the Carolina Lowcountry. Active in the community, he could not escape the Revolutionary War. As a member of the committee for the Continental Association, Walter actively recruited for the patriot cause. In 1779 he received a commission as deputy paymaster of the state militia. After the war Walter became involved with planning the Santee Canal. Although the canal was constructed after his death, he did serve as a member of a company organized in 1786 to investigate the possibility of connecting the Santee and Cooper Rivers. The president of this company was General William Moultrie, and the vice president was John Rutledge. In addition to Walter, members of the board included Generals Thomas Sumter, Francis Marion, and Charles Cotesworth Pinckney.

Walter married Ann Lesesne of Daniels Island on March 26, 1769. She died without issue that same year. On March 20, 1777, he married Ann Peyre. The union produced three daughters and a son before Ann died in 1780.

Walter was married for a third time the next year, to Dorothy Cooper. This final marriage produced one daughter.

Walter was elected to the General Assembly in the fall of 1788 but died in January 1789 before he was able to serve. He was buried in his garden on the south side of the Santee River in Berkeley County, near the old St. Stephen / St. John Parish line. DAVID H. REMBERT, JR.

Coker, W. C. "A Visit to the Grave of Thomas Walter." *Journal of Elisha Mitchell Scientific Society* 26 (April 1910): 31–42.

Maxon, William R. *Thomas Walter, Botanist.* Washington, D.C.: Smithsonian Institution, 1936.

Rembert, David. *Thomas Walter, Carolina Botanist.* Columbia: South Carolina Museum Commission, 1980.

Thomas, John Peyre, Jr. *Thomas Walter, Botanist.* Columbia: Historical Commission of South Carolina, 1946.

WASHINGTON, WILLIAM (1752–1810). Soldier. Washington was born on February 28, 1752, in Overwharton Parish, Stafford County, Virginia, the son of Bailey Washington and Catherine Storke, and he was a second cousin of President George Washington. Having no middle name, he is often confused in history with his distant cousin William Augustine Washington (1757–1810). At the outbreak of the Revolutionary War, in 1775 he was elected a captain of Stafford County Minutemen, which was integrated into the Third Virginia Regiment in 1776. After marching north with his unit later in the year, Captain Washington led a successful charge against a Hessian artillery battery at the Battle of Trenton on December 26, 1776. Wounded in this action, he was rewarded with a promotion to major of the Fourth Regiment of Continental Light Dragoons.

By the end of 1779 Washington had advanced to the rank of lieutenant colonel, commanding the Third Regiment of Continental Light Dragoons, and was ordered to join the patriot forces of General Benjamin Lincoln in Charleston, South Carolina. By March 1780 Washington's regiment was detached with the light forces near Moncks Corner to reconnoiter and screen against the advancing enemy. On March 26, 1780, he had his first encounter with British Lieutenant Colonel Banastre Tarleton near Rantowle's Bridge. Washington's command was soundly defeated by Tarleton at Moncks Corner on April 14 and again at Lenud's Ferry on May 5. After refitting in North Carolina, Washington captured Rugeley's Fort near Camden and then defeated a marauding band of Tories at Hammond's Old Store in the Little River District later in the year. On January 17, 1781, Washington commanded a combined cavalry force at the Battle of Cowpens that was instrumental in the victory there. For his intrepidity in this engagement, Congress awarded him a silver medal. Always at the head of his regiment, Washington fought valiantly at Guilford Courthouse, North Carolina, in March and, on returning to South Carolina, at Hobkirk Hill in April. At the Battle of Eutaw Springs on September 8, 1781, he was seriously wounded while leading a charge and was subsequently captured by the enemy. The British commander in the South, Lord Cornwallis, would later comment that "there could be no more formidable antagonist in a charge, at the head of his cavalry, than Colonel William Washington."

As a prisoner of war, Washington spent the remaining war years in Charleston. There he married Jane Reily Elliott on April 21, 1782, and consequently gained Sandy Hill plantation and other properties in St. Paul's Parish. The marriage produced two children. Pursuing the life of a successful Lowcountry planter, Washington represented the parish in the General Assembly from 1787 to 1804. He also accepted a post as brigadier general commanding the Seventh Brigade of state militia in 1794. During the anticipated hostilities with France in 1798, he was appointed a brigadier general in the U.S. Army commanding South Carolina and Georgia, serving until 1800. After a lingering illness, Washington died on March 16, 1810. SAMUEL K. FORE

Bailey, N. Louise, Mary L. Morgan, and Carolyn R. Taylor, eds. *Biographical Directory of the South Carolina Senate, 1776–1985.* 3 vols. Columbia: University of South Carolina Press, 1986.

Haller, Stephen E. *William Washington: Cavalryman of the Revolution.* Bowie, Md.: Heritage Books, 2001.

Lumpkin, Henry. *From Savannah to Yorktown: The American Revolution in the South.* Columbia: University of South Carolina Press, 1981.

Warley, Felix B. *An Oration, Delivered in Saint Michael's Church, in the City of Charleston, South Carolina, on Tuesday, the 19th June, 1810, on the Death of the Late Gen. William Washington.* Charleston, S.C.: W. P. Young, 1810.

WAXHAWS, BATTLE OF THE (May 29, 1780). The Battle of the Waxhaws, also known as Buford's Massacre, was one of several incidents in the backcountry that helped turn the Revolutionary War in the South into a bloody civil war. Most of Georgia and South Carolina fell under British and Loyalist control after the fall of Savannah in late 1779 and the surrender of Charleston, along with 5,500 Continentals and militiamen, on May 12, 1780.

In late May, Colonel Abraham Buford's patriot force of 350 to 400 Virginians, primarily infantry and the only significant body of Continentals remaining in the South, retreated toward North Carolina intending to join militia units there and help rebuild the American army in the Carolinas. Colonel Banastre Tarleton pursued him with a force of about 250 to 300 British regulars and Loyalists made up of cavalry, mounted infantry, and dragoons. He overtook Buford on May 29 just south of the North Carolina–South Carolina border (in present-day Lancaster County) and demanded his immediate surrender. Buford refused, and Tarleton charged the Americans, routing them. Though some Americans tried to surrender, others kept fighting, and the British and Loyalists shot or bayoneted many of them, with more than 250 killed or wounded and more than 50 taken prisoner. Tarleton later boasted, "I have cut 170 Off [ice]rs and Men to pieces." American accounts claimed that the British and Loyalists "killed at least 200 men in a most Cruel & Inhumane manner."

Most Americans considered Buford's defeat a massacre rather than a battle, and a British history of the Revolution published a few years after the war commented, "the virtue of humanity was totally forgot." This bloody action inspired many in South Carolina and elsewhere to continue, or in some cases to join, the fight against the British and Loyalists in spite of the immense odds against them. "Tarleton's Quarter!" and "Remember Buford!" became watchwords among the patriots in the southern backcountry for the rest of the war. J. TRACY POWER

Edgar, Walter. *Partisans and Redcoats: The Southern Conflict That Turned the Tide of the American Revolution.* New York: Morrow, 2001.

Lumpkin, Henry. *From Savannah to Yorktown: The American Revolution in the South.* Columbia: University of South Carolina Press, 1981.

Power, J. Tracy. "'The Virtue of Humanity Was Totally Forgot': Buford's Massacre, May 29, 1780." *South Carolina Historical Magazine* 93 (January 1992): 5–14.

WILLIAMSON, ANDREW (ca. 1730–1786). Soldier. Williamson immigrated to Ninety Six District from his native Scotland. He was earning a living as a cattle driver by 1758 and was commissioned as a lieutenant in the South Carolina Provincial Regiment of Foot during the Cherokee War of 1760–1761. At the end of the war he was awarded the contract to supply provisions to backcountry garrisons. By 1767 he had acquired a large plantation, White Hall, on Hard Labor Creek (present-day Greenwood County) and lived there with his family.

An ardent patriot at the outbreak of the Revolutionary War, Williamson held the rank of major in the militia of Ninety Six District and represented the area in the First and Second Provincial Congresses. Williamson's arrest of the Tory leader Robert Cunningham provoked British sympathizers in the region, and on November 19, 1775, a large Loyalist force attacked his patriot force, who had thrown up a hastily constructed fort at Ninety Six. After several days of intermittent fighting, both sides agreed to a truce. Reinforced by patriot soldiers under Colonel Richard Richardson, Williamson continued to pursue and detain Loyalist leaders in the following weeks in what was to become the Snow Campaign.

At the behest of William Henry Drayton, Williamson was promoted to the rank of colonel in 1776 and charged with conducting a punitive expedition against British-allied Native Americans on the frontier. The campaign subdued the Cherokees, who signed a treaty at DeWitt's Corner on May 20, 1777, that ceded practically all of their lands in South Carolina. Williamson had been promoted to the rank of brigadier general by 1778 and commanded the South Carolina militia in Major General Robert Howe's disastrous Florida expedition that summer. In September–October of the following year he participated in the unsuccessful siege of Savannah.

Williamson's actions in the days surrounding the capture of Charleston led many to conclude that he had "turned coat." He accepted British protection and retired to White Hall. Though pressed on two occasions to renounce his parole, Williamson feared for his family and accepted British protection in Charleston, where he did serve as a double agent for Continental forces. Because of this, Williamson was allowed to stay in South Carolina after the war. He died at his plantation in St. Paul's Parish, near Charleston, on March 21, 1786. SAMUEL K. FORE

Cann, Marvin L. "Prelude to War: The First Battle of Ninety-Six, November 19–21, 1775." *South Carolina Historical Magazine* 76 (October 1975): 197–214.

Johnson, Joseph. *Traditions and Reminiscences, Chiefly of the American Revolution in the South.* 1851. Reprint, Spartanburg, S.C.: Reprint Company, 1972.

Lumpkin, Henry. *From Savannah to Yorktown: The American Revolution in the South.* Columbia: University of South Carolina Press, 1981.

WILLIAMSON'S PLANTATION, BATTLE OF (July 12, 1780). After the British capture of Charleston in May 1780, many Whigs took protection and withdrew to their homes. The New Acquisition District in present-day York County was reputedly the only district in South Carolina where virtually no one took such protection from the British. In June partisan bands formed in the district and struck a Loyalist muster at Alexander's Old Fields and a garrison of Tories at Mobley's Meeting House. Lieutenant Colonel George Turnbull, commanding the British garrison at Rocky Mount, dispatched

Captain Christian Huck with a detachment of the British Legion, the New York Volunteers, and some local militia in response to these incursions. Captain Huck responded vigorously by insulting the inhabitants and pillaging the countryside. On July 11, 1780, he captured two young rebels melting pewter dishes to make bullets in the home of Captain John McClure and sentenced them to be hanged at sunrise the next day. That evening the British force encamped at the abandoned plantation of James Williamson in the community now known as Brattonsville. The location of the royal encampment reached the patriot forces that same evening. A Whig force of 133 men under the command of Colonels William Bratton, William Hill, Edward Lacey, and Andrew Neel and Captain James McClure resolved to march on the British camp and attack at first light. Dividing their forces in two, the rebels encircled the enemy camp and attacked. Caught by surprise, Huck's force of about 120 troops offered little resistance. An American sharpshooter felled Captain Huck. Casualties were fairly high for the British troops. However, the Americans only suffered one killed. Popularly known as Huck's Defeat, the Battle of Williamson's Plantation was the first significant check on the British advance since their victory at Charleston.   SAMUEL K. FORE

Edgar, Walter. *Partisans and Redcoats: The Southern Conflict That Turned the Tide of the American Revolution.* New York: Morrow, 2001.

Scoggins, Michael. "Huck's Defeat: The Battle of Williamson's Plantation." Serialized in *York County Genealogical & Historical Society Quarterly* 13–14 (September 2001–March 2003).

Thomas, Samuel N. *The Dye Is Cast: The Scots-Irish and Revolution in the Carolina Back Country.* Columbia, S.C.: Palmetto Conservation Foundation, 1997.

WRAGG, WILLIAM (ca. 1714–1777). Loyalist. Wragg was born in South Carolina, the son of Samuel Wragg and Marie DuBosc. His father was a prosperous merchant and influential member of the Royal Council. William benefited from his father's wealth and influence and was educated in England at Westminster, St. John's College, Oxford, and the Middle Temple. Called to the English Bar in 1733, he practiced law until he returned to South Carolina about the time of his father's death. In England he married Mary Wood, and the union produced one son. Mary Wragg died in 1767, and William married his cousin Henrietta Wragg on February 5, 1769. His second marriage produced four children.

When Samuel Wragg died in 1750, William inherited substantial property, including the 6,000-acre Ashley Barony, a Charleston townhouse, 6,900 acres on the Pee Dee River, and three plantations: River Settlement, Middle Settlement, and Wampee. In 1777 Wragg's estate included 7,100 acres and 256 slaves with an appraised value of £36,359 sterling.

Wragg continued his father's tradition of public service. Named to the Royal Council in 1753, he supported the council in its controversies with the Commons House over the tax bill. Wragg became the spokesman for the council and for the crown as the ultimate source of authority. Ironically, in an attempt to appease the Commons House, Governor William Henry Lyttleton asked the crown to suspend Wragg because of his vociferous support of the crown. On December 6, 1757, Wragg was suspended, and he was later removed.

In 1758 St. John's Colleton Parish elected Wragg to the Commons House of Assembly, where he would represent the parish until 1768. He declined further service because he did not support the Massachusetts and Virginia Resolutions. St. Helena's Parish elected him in 1773, but again he refused to serve. During his time in the Commons House, Wragg consistently supported the prerogatives of the British crown. He opposed the actions of the Stamp Act Congress. In 1769 he published "Reasons for Not Concurring in the Non-Importation Resolution" in the *South-Carolina Gazette.* He also protested the erection of a statue honoring William Pitt, suggesting one of King George III instead. In 1769 Wragg declined appointment as chief justice for South Carolina because he did not wish to profit from his devotion to the crown. He also declined reappointment to the Royal Council.

In 1775 Wragg refused to sign the Non-Importation Association or to recognize the authority of the Continental Congress. Confined to his plantation, Wragg refused to take an oath of abjuration in 1777. Banished from South Carolina, Wragg left his wife and daughters and sailed for Amsterdam in July. On September 2, 1777, his ship, the *Commerce,* foundered off the coast of Holland. Wragg drowned trying to save the life of his son.

The English honored Wragg's loyalty with a tablet in his memory—the first erected for an American. Now in Westminster Abbey, the inscription is a fitting tribute to his devotion to England: "In Him, Strong natural Parts, improved by Education, together with Love of Justice and Humanity, Formed the compleat character of A Good Man." ALEXIA JONES HELSLEY

Edgar, Walter B., and N. Louise Bailey, eds. *Biographical Directory of the South Carolina House of Representatives.* Vol. 2, *The Commons House of Assembly, 1692–1775.* Columbia: University of South Carolina Press, 1977.

ZUBLY, JOHN JOACHIM (August 27, 1724–July 23, 1781). Minister. John J. Zubly was born in St. Gall, Switzerland, to Reformed Protestants David and Helena Zubly. While Zubly was still a gymnasium student, his parents left in 1736 for the Swiss immigrant enclave at Purrysburg in South Carolina before settling in Georgia. Zubly set out to join them after his ordination at London's German Reformed Church on August 19, 1744.

Zubly preached for a time among the Salzburger community, where he met Anna Tobler, whom he married on November 12, 1746. They had one child, who died. His second wife was Ann (Pye?). The Reformed congregation in Vernonsburg, near Savannah, petitioned the Georgia trustees to appoint Zubly as their pastor the congregation then chose another, who remained even after the trustees finally approved Zubly's appointment. Zubly then traveled among German communities in the South Carolina Lowcountry and Georgia, preaching whenever possible there and among the German Lutheran community in Orangeburg. In 1757 he accepted a call to pastor the Wappetaw Church on Wando Neck northeast of Charleston. Known for his erudition, Zubly occasionally lectured at the Independent Meeting House in Charleston and in 1759 published a collection of sermons dealing with a Calvinist understanding of the meaning of death. Later he wrote in opposition to the appointment of an Anglican bishop for the colonies. His learning led the College of New Jersey (Princeton) to confer on him both M.A. and D.D. degrees.

Zubly, however, is noted more for his political writings and involvement in public affairs, which came in 1760 after he accepted a call to the Independent Church in Savannah. There he also acquired considerable land and slaves. As tension between the colonies and Britain intensified following passage of the Stamp Act in 1765, Zubly penned several tracts sketching for a Georgia audience inclined to Loyalist sentiment various perspectives emerging in colonial political circles. Consequently, in July 1775 he was elected to the Georgia provincial congress and then selected to represent Georgia in the Continental Congress.

Although Zubly appreciated colonial opposition to British imperial policy, some of which he believed was oppressive, he remained convinced that nothing should sever ties between colonies and mother country. Hence he opposed moves toward independence, returning to Savannah in October 1775. With independence sentiment in Georgia growing, Zubly was branded a Loyalist, taken into custody by the Georgia Committee of Public Safety, and in late 1777 banished from Georgia, with much of his estate confiscated.

Zubly came to South Carolina, but he returned to Savannah in 1779 after the reestablishment of a royal colonial government. Distrusted by both ardent patriots and Loyalists, Zubly remained in Savannah until his death. He is buried in Savannah's Colonial Park. CHARLES LIPPY

Hawes, Lilla Mills, ed. *Journal of the Reverend John Joachim Zubly, A.M. D.D., March 5, 1770 through June 22, 1781.* Savannah: Georgia Historical Society, 1989.

Martin, Roger A. "John J. Zubly: Preacher, Planter, and Politician." Ph.D. diss., University of Georgia, 1976.

Miller, Randall M., ed. *"A Warm & Zealous Spirit": John J. Zubly and the American Revolution, a Selection of His Writings.* Macon, Ga.: Mercer University Press, 1982.

Seamon, Janice Louise. "John Joachim Zubly: A Voice for Liberty and Principle." M.A. thesis, University of South Carolina, 1982.